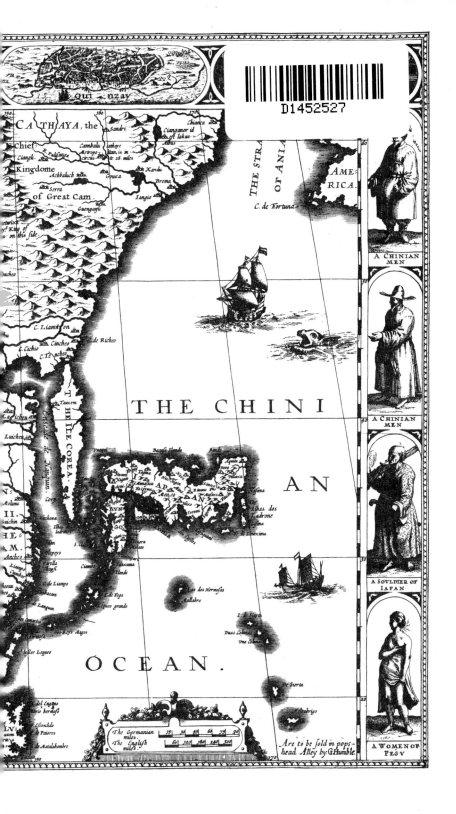

A
CYCLE
OF
CATHAY

A
CYCLE
OF
CATHAY

*The Chinese Vogue in England
during the Seventeenth and
Eighteenth Centuries*

by

WILLIAM W. APPLETON

OCTAGON BOOKS

A DIVISION OF FARRAR, STRAUS AND GIROUX

New York   1979

Copyright 1951 Columbia University Press, New York

Reprinted 1979
by special arrangement with Columbia University Press

OCTAGON BOOKS
A DIVISION OF FARRAR STRAUS & GIROUX, INC.
19 Union Square West
New York, N.Y. 10003

Library of Congress Cataloging in Publication Data

Appleton, William Worthen.
    A cycle of Cathay.

    Originally presented as the author's thesis, Columbia University.
    Reprint of the ed. published by Columbia University Press, New
    York.
    Includes bibliographical references and index.
    1. China—Relations (general) with Great Britain.   2. Great Britain
    —Relations (general) with China.   I. Title.
[DS740.5.G5A7   1979]   301.29'51'042   78-15422
ISBN 0-374-90277-1

Manufactured by Braun-Brumfield, Inc.
Ann Arbor, Michigan
Printed in the United States of America

PREFACE

*W*HEN TENNYSON WROTE "Better fifty years of Europe than a cycle of Cathay," he was voicing both nineteenth century England's optimism and its exasperation with the static and reactionary policies of China. The times were moving, but the Manchu emperors refused to move along with them. The unsatisfactory trade relations between the two countries may have in part prompted his observation. It was probably also a reflection of the prevailing intellectual temper. During the seventeenth and eighteenth centuries a mythical China had been created. Largely a synthetic product, the China that Stuart and Augustan Englishmen visualized was seen refracted through Jesuit eyes; it was associated with the artistry of Chippendale, the wit of Goldsmith, and the deistic worship of Confucius. Few were the British voyagers who brought back firsthand accounts, and fewer still were the genuine Sinologists. As the disparities between the myth and the actuality became apparent, the reaction set in. Enthusiasm dwindled to bewilderment and irritation and, ultimately, to downright hostility.

For a study of this cycle the year 1600 serves as an approximate starting point, marking as it does the founding of the East India Company. The failure of the English embassy to China at the end of the eighteenth century brackets its close. Between these dates the Chinese legend slowly grew, flourished briefly, and died lingeringly. Its effects upon English life and letters were spasmodic and various. So scattered were these manifestations that it is virtually impossible to treat them chronologically.

Of the native Chinese scholars engaged in such studies in Occidental universities, a greater part have used the chronological method, but the results have not always been altogether satisfactory. Their collections of scattered references to China sometimes seem more like kaleidoscopic patterns than clear and orderly mosaics. Consequently, it has seemed to me preferable to marshal these references more or less thematically, with the chapters in approximately chronological order, corresponding to the flowering of interest in these individual aspects of the Chinese vogue.

Primarily, I have been concerned with English interest in China. Continental aspects of Sinology have already received much attention. The work of Cordier, Reichwein, and Martino is too well known to need comment. The part which China played in developing the ideas of Leibniz, Voltaire and the French deists has been considerably discussed elsewhere, and scholars continue to explore its French and German manifestations. Justifiably, the emphasis in these seventeenth and eighteenth century studies has been on China's importance for Europe. The cosmopolitanism of Goldsmith was certainly far shallower than that of the Marquis d'Argens, and the intellectual foment stirred up by China on the continent far more intense than that across the Channel. In more ways than one English interest was curiously insular.

To trace the graph of this interest in England and to outline its broad patterns, since no book has as yet appeared on this subject, is the purpose of this study. Individual aspects remain to be examined in more detail. The importance of Confucius has yet to be thoroughly discussed, despite Arnold H. Rowbotham's spadework in this respect. The important studies of B. Sprague Allen and Arthur O. Lovejoy will doubtless lead to further exploration of the Chinese influence in the history of taste and the history of ideas.

Within the last decade interest in these problems has been

enormously stimulated. In addition to research in the seventeenth and eighteenth centuries, comparative studies on Chinese thought and letters and the English Romantic Poets have attracted much notice. Almost certainly, such attention will increase. The cross-fertilization of cultures is a rich and complex process. It is my hope that this study will in some measure contribute to the heightening of this interest.

In conclusion, I wish to thank Marjorie H. Nicolson and Norman Torrey for their help in the preparation of this book, L. Carrington Goodrich for his many helpful suggestions, and, in particular, James L. Clifford for his patience, encouragement, and guidance.

W.W.A.

August, 1950
New York

CONTENTS

ILLUSTRATIONS

A
CYCLE
OF
CATHAY

I

MERCHANT AND

MISSIONARY

$\mathcal{T}$HE LONG VOYAGE HOME from the courts of the Great Khan was over. Clad in their ragged Tartar clothes, so the story goes, three men confronted the disbelieving Venetians who had long since given them up for dead. Only when the travelers had summoned the skeptics to a banquet and, slitting the lining of their beggarly dress, allowed a rain of jewels to cascade to the floor, were the onlookers convinced that the three Polos had finally returned. The name which the dazzled Venetians bestowed upon the youngest of them symbolized for Europe the splendor of the East—Marco, Il Milione.[1]

The Mediterranean world had, indeed, enjoyed some contact with the East centuries earlier.[2] Tradition tells of an Egyptian embassy to China some twelve centuries before Christ.[3] The Greeks and Romans had a fragmentary knowledge of a distant land of exquisite silks.[4] Such information and

[1] Sir Henry Yule, *The Book of Ser Marco Polo*, 2d ed. (London, 1875), I, 4–5; Eileen Power, *Medieval People*, London, 1924, Ch. II.

[2] Early Sino-European contacts are discussed in the following: Sir Henry Yule, *Cathay and the Way Thither*, London, 1913–16; Adolf Reichwein, *China and Europe*, New York, 1925; Friedrich Hirth, *China and the Roman Orient*, Shanghai, 1885; Arnold H. Rowbotham, "A Brief Account of the Early Development of Sinology," *Chinese Social and Political Science Review*, VII, No. 2 (April, 1923), 113–38; Ch'en Shou-yi, "Sino-European Cultural Contacts since the Discovery of the Sea Route," *Nankai Social and Economic Quarterly*, VIII, No. 1 (April, 1935), 44–74. The greatest bibliography both for this period and later Sinological literature is Henri Cordier's *Biblioteca Sinica*, Paris, 1904–24.

[3] Yule, *Cathay*, I, 10.

[4] See sections 1 and 2 in the preliminary essay to Yule's *Cathay*. Also Hirth, *China and the Roman Orient*; George Coedès, *Textes d'auteurs*

such contacts were, however, ephemeral, and it was not until Jenghiz, as Khan of the Mongols, conquered North China in 1215, that the first real period of Sino-European relations began.

The subsequent rise to power of the Mongol dynasty shook the European Continent, and though a succession of accidents combined to prevent an invasion of the Western world, the specter of the inundating hordes haunted the West. When Kublai Khan consolidated the conquest of China two ways to exorcise these fears suggested themselves: the merchants of the Near East by extending their trade routes to the edges of the world hoped to bring civilization to the Far Eastern barbarians; churchmen, on the other hand, fevered by the legend of Prester John, the Christian monarch of a kingdom somewhere west of China, had a still greater dream—the conversion of the Great Khan.[5]

Though the hopes of the merchants were in part realized when the trade routes to Cathay became established during the thirteenth century, the dreams of the ecclesiastics proved more visionary. John of Plano Carpini's exhausting overland voyage in 1246 to the court of the Great Khan failed dismally.[6] His conciliatory letter from the Holy Father elicited no more than the Khan's haughty and unsatisfactory suggestion that the Pope acknowledge his submission to the Emperor of the East. The embassy seven years later of William of Rubruck from St. Louis of France failed equally to impress the Khan with

---

grecs et latins relatifs a l'extrême orient depuis le IVe siècle avant J-C. jusqu'au XIVe siècle, Paris, 1910.

[5]The legend of Prester John is discussed in Volume III of Yule's Cathay and in Karl A. Wittfogel and Fêng Chia-shêng, History of Chinese Society (New York, 1949), pp. 639–40.

[6]Richard Hakluyt, Principal Navigations Voyages Traffiques & Discoveries (Glasgow, 1903), I, 55–179. An authoritative text of Carpini's account is published in the Hakluyt Society, n. s., Vol. IV (London, 1900), 1–32. Paul Pelliot states that the best translation is that by Friedrich Risch published in Leipzig in 1930.

the glories of the See of Rome.[7] By the time of Friar Odoric of Pordenone's expedition in 1323, the conversion of the Mongol emperor seemed no nearer at hand.[8]

Despite the failure of these missionaries to accomplish their purpose, they blazed a path for travelers, and they bequeathed to Europe a series of notable narratives. Understandably, they approached the East with a mixture of fear and wonder, and though they attempted realistic travel journals, they were unable to sustain consistently a disinterested attitude. The account of Friar Odoric perhaps the most interesting of these narratives, is typica in this respect. Occupied at one moment with a painstaking computation of Quinzai's 10,002 bridges, a moment later he is giving full rein to his imagination. He loses himself among the pomposities and splendors of the court of the Khan; he tells of a mountain snow-white upon one side and coal-black upon the other; he spins legends of the Old Man of the Mountain; he marvels at the Circe-like garden in which he found 4200 human souls imprisoned in the bodies of cats and apes.[9]

It was to this account and those of William of Rubruck and John of Plano Carpini that the prince of literary impostors turned.[10] Sir John Mandeville's *Travels*, a synthesis of fables and wonders, published in England by Wynkyn de Worde in 1499, but known on the Continent even earlier, so captivated Europe that it eclipsed even the popularity of Polo's account until comparatively recent times. By the end of the seventeenth century Mandeville's work had enjoyed nine English editions. With Marco Polo's narrative it stimulated the first

[7]William of Rubruck's narrative is published in the Hakluyt Society, n. s., IV (London, 1900), 40 ff. There is also considerable mention of Rubruck in Yule's *Cathay*, Vol. I.

[8]Yule, *Cathay*, Vol. II. See also Henri Cordier, *Les Voyages en Asie au XIVe siècle du bienhereux frère Odoric de Pordenone*, Paris, 1891.

[9]Hakluyt, *Principal Navigations*, IV, 427 ff.

[10]Sir John Mandeville, *Travels*, ed. A. W. Pollard, London, 1905.

real interest in China. The appeal both books made was not primarily intellectual. It was above all imaginative. Polo's account was a romance of the court of Kublai Khan. The narrative shifted from the glories of his palaces and pavilions to his tumultuous carouses and festivals and the savage barbarities of the hunts that Marco so much enjoyed. It conjured up a vision of the court of Kembalu with its astrologers and magicians. The appeal of Mandeville's book was similar. He plundered his sources with zest, taking the raw material of the missionary narratives and weaving it into a tapestry of fantasy and fact. He envisioned a celestial city and court and transmuted the scene with the opulence of a Midas. So absorbed did he become, in fact, in chronicling the wonders of jeweled thrones and pilasters and cunningly contrived golden peacocks that seemed to dance, that he found little time to mention the more mundane aspects of Chinese life.[11] Though he called attention to the Great Khan's philosopher-advisers, his system of couriers to relay provincial reports,[12] and made some casual observations on the laws and customs of the Tartars in Cathay,[13] essentially he was writing a fantasy, an early *Vathek*. His narration, like that of Polo, and to some extent those of the early missionaries, belongs in essence to the literature of wonder.

The second period of Sinological literature differed sharply from this.[14] The fall of the Mongol dynasty in 1368 severed

---

[11]Cf. Mandeville, *Travels*, Chs. XXII and XXIII, with Odoric's account in Hakluyt, *Principal Navigations*, IV, 422–30.

[12]Chapter XXV in Mandeville is again a virtual paraphrase of Odoric.

[13]Chapter XXVI in Mandeville is largely a composite of material from John of Plano Carpini and William of Rubruck.

[14]See Cordier's *Bibliotheca Sinica*. See also Pierre Martino, *L'Orient dans la litterature française au XVIIe et XVIIIe siècle*, Paris, 1906; Arnold H. Rowbotham, *Missionary and Mandarin*, Berkeley, Calif., 1942; Virgile Pinot, *La Chine et la formation de l'esprit philosophique en France, 1640–1740*, Paris, 1932; Louis J. Gallagher, *The China That Was*, Milwaukee, Wis., 1942.

China's relations with the West. The caravans of the missionaries and traders no longer rolled over the snow-swept wastes and blazing deserts. But Europe had not forgotten the riches and wonders of the East. At the dawn of the sixteenth century the star of the Portuguese empire was in the ascendant, and under Prince Henry the Navigator and John II its bounds stretched eastward as far as Ormuz, Socotra, and Goa. By 1514 a trade embassy had been dispatched from Lisbon to the court of the Mings, and three years later Thomas Pirez set foot in Canton as an ambassador.[15] Accompanied by a richly dressed retinue, he was well received after a dramatic debarkation to the sounds of trumpets and cannon. But the Emperor was unprepared for this invasion. The triumphant arrival in Peking culminated in a charge of espionage, Pirez' ignominious dismissal, and his imprisonment and death.[16] The Chinese, with their profound xenophobia, resented his invasion of their self-sufficient empire.

Their concern would have been far more acute had they known how much more dangerous an adversary was shortly to arrive on their threshold. In 1541, at the instigation of John III, Francis Xavier set sail from Lisbon to convert the Eastern world.[17] For ten years he sailed from Mozambique to India, Malacca, and Japan, but his consuming desire was the conversion of the mightiest empire of the East. In the autumn of the eleventh year of his travels he died, within sight of his goal, on the rocky island of Sancian near Canton. Though his most ardent wish remained unfulfilled, his successors were determined to realize it. Their hopes were furthered by the

[15]Juan de Mendoza, *History of the Great and Mighty Kingdom of China,* ed. Sir George Staunton, Hakluyt Society, XIV (1853–54), xxxi ff. The Pirez embassy has also been described by Paul Pelliot in *T'oung Pao,* XXXVIII (1948), 81 ff.

[16]Samuel Purchas, *Hakluytus Posthumus; or, Purchas His Pilgrimes* (Glasgow, 1906), XII, 100. Mendoza, *History of . . . China,* pp. xxxvi.

[17]Rowbotham, *Missionary and Mandarin,* Ch. III.

fact that Portuguese merchantmen, for their help in sweeping the South China coast free of pirates, were granted reluctant permission to settle on Macao, a peninsula below Canton, on the west side of the Canton River. By 1563 Macao had some 700 Portuguese residents and had become the port of entry both for their merchants and missionaries and for the travelers sailing northward from the Spanish colonies in the Philippines.[18] Inspired by the dreams of Xavier, the Jesuits established a station there. In 1578 Father Alexander Valignanus and Father Michael Ruggierius arrived to set the stage for the Jesuit invasion, but it was with the debarkation of Father Ricci in 1582 that the Jesuit foothold in China was solidly established.[19]

A man of brilliant mind and unbounded energy, he set the pattern for his successors. No sooner had he touched land than he set about learning Chinese. Keenly perceptive, he soon realized that stability for the church could be obtained only through the Emperor's interest, and consequently he centered his plans on penetration of the Celestial City. The story of his expedition there, some years later, reads like a comic epic.

After a series of false starts Ricci finally succeeded in reaching Peking in 1598, but the all-important court eunuchs, disappointed in their hopes that he would teach them alchemy, embarrassed him by a trumped-up charge of espionage and forced his return to Nanking where he was subjected to the

[18]Ibid., p. 50. Much has been recently written on Macao: Henri Bernard, *Monumenta Serica*, VII, 288–94; Charles R. Boxer, *Fidalgos in the Far East, 1550–1770; Fact and Fancy in the History of Macao*, The Hague, 1948.

[19]There is a wealth of material on Ricci. See Rowbotham, *Missionary and Mandarin*, Ch. IV; Nicholas Trigault, *De Christiana expeditione apud Sinas suscepta ab Societate Jesu*, Amsterdam, 1615; Gallagher, *The China That Was*; Maurice Collis, *The Great Within*, London, 1942; "The Jesuits in the Far East," Purchas, *Hakluytus Posthumus*, XII, 239–331; F. Alvarez Semedo, *The History of That Great and Renowned Monarchy of China* (London, 1655), pp. 172 ff.

interminable delays of Chinese officialdom. Eventually he set out once more, laden with gifts, only to encounter again a "covetous capon" who delayed his progress by charging him with witchcraft and sedition. An imperial summons extricated him from this difficulty. The Emperor ordered him back to the capital where the novelty of the clavichord, clocks, and religious pictures which Ricci had brought found temporary favor in the royal eyes. The Emperor's curiosity soon evaporated, however, and the cause of the church was not substantially advanced. The missionary gift-bearer was not granted an audience. The eunuchs and Board of Rites quarreled over his official status, but as time dragged on he remained in Peking. The court functionaries vainly memorialized a disinterested Emperor, and, when the tiresome question of status was ultimately dropped, Ricci could reflect with satisfaction that he had attained at least a part of his objective. He was permitted to settle in Peking for the remainder of his life.

He died in 1610 without ever having been presented before the Dragon Throne, but during the long wait he made valuable contacts with some of the leading officials. To his great joy, a few even espoused the foreign religion. In his disputations with them he was, nonetheless, troubled. He found their concern with scientific learning, astronomy, mathematics, hydraulics, and optics far greater than their interest in religious problems. The Jesuit College had fortified Father Ricci both with sound theological doctrine and a firm grasp of the sciences, but left unanswered a delicate question. To what extent was a missionary justified in concentrating on the secular aspects of Jesuit education in hope of arousing the interest of the unconverted? Was he, in short, to stress the role of priest or scholar?

Ricci's answer to this question had the gravest consequences, and ultimately plunged the Catholic world into the schismatic

Rites quarrel.[20] Opportunistic as his decision may have been, there was much to vindicate his choice of the scholar's role. The governing class who, in the course of the examinations for magistracies, committed the accumulated wisdom of China to heart, and whose lives were steeped in perfected traditions, viewed the strangers from the West with a curiosity that would have turned to immediate hostility at any suspicion of a direct assault on the state religion of Confucianism. Xavier's method of proselytizing, Ricci realized, would only provoke disaster. To assume ragged clothes, ring a bell, collect a crowd and preach, would be the sheerest folly. Ricci decided on a more indirect approach. The worlds both of the Mings and Aquinas were predicated on the concept of a static body of knowledge, and through their amalgamation into a new *Summa*, perhaps, Ricci hoped to convince the Chinese of their pagan errors. He resolved, therefore, to assimilate as much of the Confucian doctrine as possible into the Catholic dogma. Diplomatically, he decided to proselytize among the upper classes on the grounds that the adoption of Christianity by the ruling class would facilitate mass—or even national—conversion. The specter of the land of Prester John still haunted the Jesuits.

Time vindicated in large measure Ricci's policy. Under his leadership the missionary dropped the garb of the priest or bonze, a class popularly held in contempt, and assumed that of the scholar. This fact alone is of inestimable importance, for it led to the selection of missionaries who were not only theologically robust but thoroughly trained in the sciences and capable of acute observation. The promise of Ricci's dying words, "I leave you facing an open door,"[21] was filled by a growing succession of colleagues, despite the conquest of

[20]Rowbotham, *Missionary and Mandarin*, Chs. IX–XII; Antonio S. Rosso, *Apostolic Legations to China of the Eighteenth Century*, 1948.

[21]Quoted in Rowbotham, *Missionary and Mandarin*, p. 66.

China by the Manchus.[22] The Ming empire succumbed to internal decay and the foreign invader, but the new Manchu dynasty found places at court for the Jesuit scholars. Shun Chih was quick to discover how useful they could be both in such trifling occupations as repairing spinets and composing Chinese airs, or in more important projects such as surveying, making maps, and founding cannon. Their knowledge of astronomy likewise proved invaluable in the reform of the calendar, and on several occasions saved the lives of the missionaries in trials of skill with rival Chinese and Mohammedan astronomers. So impressive did these tests prove that Father Verbiest, outsider though he was, was appointed director of the Bureau of Astronomy.[23]

Persecutions and edicts notwithstanding, the cause of the church was advancing. Little by little the Portuguese and Spanish Jesuits found occasion also to advance their national causes. The merchants of Macao feared European competitors and the possible loss of a profitable market, and the highly placed missionaries were in an ideal position to help determine the tides of royal favor. Their skill in manipulation checkmated at least one menace. The Dutch, since the establishment of their own East India Company in 1602 and the seizure of the Spice Islands and Malay Peninsula, had looked longingly toward the Chinese mainland.[24] But their hopes were transitory. Their commercial embassies to the Emperor were, it appears, so successfully undermined by the missionaries of rival empires, that, though they later were conceded factories in Canton, they centered their attention on trade with Japan.

[22]*Bellum Tartaricum; or, The Conquest of China by the Tartars,* tr. from the Latin of Martin Martinius, London, 1655. The later history of the missions is well covered in the sources mentioned in note 19.

[23]Two letters from Father Verbiest are given in the *Philosophical Transactions of the Royal Society,* XVI (March–April, 1686), 35–62.

[24]Jan J. L. Duyvendak is the authority on Dutch Sinological literature and cultural contacts. See *T'oung Pao,* XXXII (1936), 293–344.

The Portuguese and Spanish faced a still more dangerous adversary, however. English interest in the rich silk and spice trade had long been keen.[25] Attempts to establish sea routes to Cathay were made as early as 1497, when John Cabot, a mariner of Italian birth who appreciated the value of Oriental trade, sought the Northwest Passage. The sixteenth century abounded with similar seekers—John Cabot's son Sebastian, Sir Hugh Willoughby, Anthony Jenkinson, and Frobisher. Though their ports were thrown open to the British by trade agreements in 1576, the Portuguese were in no hurry to facilitate their rival's trade with the Orient. Early accounts of the East filtering back to Europe had extolled its size and wealth, and practical British merchants detected a vast potential market for English wool.[26] Ludovico Georgio's map of China (published in Antwerp in 1584, and the earliest map of China in the British Museum) reflects the increasing attention paid to that country. It is revealed also in Queen Elizabeth's letter of 1583 to the Emperor, commending to him her servant John Newbery, and deferentially but firmly urging the advantages of mutual traffic.[27] Unfortunately the project came to nothing. A second attempt to establish relations proved hardly more satisfactory.[28] Organized by Sir Robert Dudley, a mission sailed bravely out in 1596 under the command of Benjamin Wood in the picturesquely named *Beare, Beares Whelp,* and *Benjamin.* Their subsequent history is a mystery. An intercepted letter mentions the capture of a Spanish treasure ship, but the mission never saw England again, and

[25]Earl H. Pritchard, *Anglo-Chinese Relations during the Seventeenth and Eighteenth Centuries* (University of Illinois, 1929), pp. 42–44.

[26]Hosea B. Morse, *The Chronicles of the East India Company Trading to China, 1635–1834* (Oxford, 1926), I, 6–8; Pritchard, *Anglo-Chinese Relations,* p. 45; Dedication to Parke's translation of Mendoza, *History of . . . China,* London, 1588.

[27]Hakluyt, *Principal Navigations,* V, 451–52.

[28]*Ibid.,* XI, 417–21.

only a few broken planks found drifting in the West Indian seas hinted at its end.[29]

Such disappointments seemed merely to whet English anxiety to develop the Eastern markets. By 1600 the British East India Company had been organized. Despite an un-remunerative first trip to the Orient, a second venture in 1604 returned a 95 percent profit.[30] From that moment on, the value of trade with the Far East was firmly established in the minds of those who were more swayed by balance sheets than by liter-ary accounts. By 1617 the company had established twelve Oriental factories, and though the subsequent English trade in China was restricted almost entirely to the ports of Amoy and Macao, during the century to come the tonnage and the profits slowly mounted. Commercial as the ventures may have been, the cargoes which these ships carried were those of high romance: *Verzino*, quicksilver, lignum aloes, cubeb, amomum, galangae, musk, silks, and pearls as big as doves' eggs.[31] The golden age of Drake and Hawkins was over, but such inventories fired the imagination of the English. It spurred them beyond the pillars of Hercules toward Ultima Thule. It precipitated Ralph Fitch into the horrors of the inquisition at Goa. It brought the meteoric rise to power of Samuel White in Siam. It drove Peter Mundy on his mission with Captain Weddell to the coasts of China.[32]

At the time of this voyage English prestige in the Orient was still at a low ebb. The 1623 massacre of the British in Amboina was unavenged. Government policy was weak, and

[29]Purchas, *Hakluytus Posthumus*, XII, 218–19, and II, 288–97. Hakluyt, *Principal Navigations*, XI, 2.

[30]Pritchard, *Anglo-Chinese Relations*, p. 48.

[31]Hakluyt, *Principal Navigations*, VI, 25–27, and IX, 392.

[32]*The Travels of Peter Mundy in Europe and Asia*, ed. Sir Richard Temple, The Hakluyt Society, ser. II, Vols. XLV–XLVI, London, 1919. These constitute Vol. III, Parts I and II of Mundy's *Travels*. See also Morse, *Chronicles*, I, 14–30; James B. Eames, *The English in China* (London, 1909), pp. 12–22.

interlopers such as Sir Edward Michelborne troubled the trade routes. Nonetheless, the vision of the wealth of the Indies had not faded. It was only natural that in the hope of refurbishing his always depleted treasury, Charles I and his favorite, Endymion Porter, sanctioned Sir William Courteen's venture to establish free trade with China.

Under the command of Captain John Weddell, with whom Mundy served, the *Dragon, Catherine,* and *Sun* and their accompanying pinnaces left England in 1636. They sailed eastward to Goa, to Singapore, and finally to Macao. Once arrived, they found negotiations tediously slow. Alarmed at the prospects of rivalry, the Portuguese were not eager to assist the English in negotiating with the Chinese authorities. Delays and interminable protocol blocked them at every turn. Captain Weddell fumed with exasperation, and the presence in the port of a Spanish galleon laden with treasure made the English crew restless. Finally Weddell's impatience led him to attempt a direct approach to the officials at Canton, unaware that tradition forbade attempts of this kind. In the course of these enforced negotiations with port officials Chinese fireboats suddenly appeared and bore down on the British ships. Weddell's fleet miraculously escaped disaster but the English, infuriated at this unexpected attack, angrily cruised up the river, blew up a fort, burned some junks, and raided villages. These actions brought results that weeks of negotiation failed to achieve, and the Chinese authorities, in their anxiety to close the incident as quickly as possible, agreed to allow certain trading privileges contingent on the immediate departure of the English. The expedition thus achieved some measure of success,[33] though Captain Weddell perished with all hands on board the *Dragon* during the return trip through the Indian Ocean.

When the surviving ships touched England again, Mundy

[33]Morse, *Chronicles,* I, 25–26.

added the tale to his already substantial travel narratives. The story as he tells it has a realistic simplicity and directness. As an alert and inquisitive traveler whose interests ranged from white porpoises and green pigeons to tangled linguistic problems, he logged the trip scrupulously, recording wonders and rarities in his sketchbook, sight-seeing indefatigably whenever the ship touched land. His account of the Cantonese adventure is consequently that of an acute observer.

His attitude toward China was from the outset mixed. Like so many of the early travelers, he was immediately impressed by the Chinese xenophobia, cowardice, and greed. In describing the English journey unmolested up the river among a hostile fleet, he remarked, "For such is their Cowardize, that though each of these vessells was as well furnished with ordnance as the *Annes,* and treble mannd, yet durst they not all to oppose hir in any hostile way."[34] On a shore trip to buy provisions for the ship, he found among the Chinese a greed for silver sufficient even to overcome their distrust.[35] The pagan altars and idols attracted his rapt attention as they did that of other travelers. He made note of divining sticks, goldfish, dramatic performances, and various other aspects of Chinese life, and concluded his brief sketch with an account of China's religion and excellencies which is worth quoting in full, so truly does it mirror the spirit of contemporary accounts.

After observing that religion was little respected, and in some instances not professed at all, he added:

Of the Religion off the Chinois I cannott speake much. Only I mett one who told mee hee was of thatt secte thatt beelieved No other then this liffe; very curious in adorning their Pagodes, wherin are the Images off those they accompte For saintes, allthough they shew No greatt respect to the place Nor them, For they will talke,

[34] Mundy, *Travels,* III, Part I, 179.
[35] *Ibid.*, p. 189.

eatt, Drincke, walcke and play in their pagodes and before their altars as in a commons house, For as much as I saw.[36]

Of China's excellencies he remarked:

This Countrie May be said to excell in these particulers: Antiquity, largeness, Ritcheness, healthynesse, Plentiffullnesse. For Arts and manner off governmentt I thinck noe Kingdome in the world Comparable to it. Considered alltogether.[37]

Curiously, on this last point Mundy failed to elaborate. It is even stranger that he should have made the assertion in view of the unsatisfactory official relations of the expedition. But his remark is typical and is echoed again and again in contemporary and later narratives. It was only with the later Jesuits that China was to be applauded for her moral perfections; earlier, it is her good government which is stressed. China was developed in the popular imagination as a land ripe for profitable exploitation. Large, rich, and peaceful—what more admirable combination could be conceived?

A narrative such as Mundy's, which in so many ways reads like a composite of those of the Portuguese and Spanish travelers, is typical of the second class of early literature on China. To the literature of wonder, this second type, the more factual narrative succeeded. Even the writings of the early Jesuits, Ricci, Trigault, and Martinius, were for the most part far more objective than the paeans of their immediate successors. In this second group of Sinological literature we find rich and comparatively unexplored tracts: Perera's *Certaine Reports* (translated in 1577 in Eden's *History of Travayle in the West and East Indies*), Bernardino de Escalante's *Discourse of the Navigation Which the Portugales Doe Make to the Realmes and Provinces of the East Partes of the World,* Juan Gonzales de Mendoza's *History of China* (1588), and the

[36]*Ibid.,* pp. 301–302.   [37]*Ibid.,* p. 303.

narratives of Alvarez Semedo, Fernam Mendez Pinto, Trigault, and Martinius. They write with a wandering luxuriance and analyze Chinese morals and aspects of government with the objectivity of an alien spectator. Though not individually familiar to the Elizabethan common reader, these works, condensed and macaronically assembled in Hakluyt and Purchas, were brought before a comparatively wide audience.

Embedded in the vast matrix of Hakluyt, the dialogue between three Portuguese at Macao is typical of these accounts.[38] Using the didactic conversational device, it discusses the geography of the provinces of China, its Great Wall, its various sorts of cities, and vast river population. The author remains on his guard against too encomiastic a description and warns against the current opinion that famine, war, and pestilence have not afflicted China: "But that opinion is more common then true: sithens there have been most terrible intestine and civile warres,"[39] in addition to periodic visitations by other Apocalyptic horsemen. The riches of the country, the artificers, and habits of dress he next considers; and their styles of magistrates, "the principal cause of their tranquillity and peace," he considerably praises. On the other hand, the author counters this praise by dismissing Chinese knowledge in liberal sciences and natural and moral philosophy as negligible.

Throughout the essay the balance swings first in favor of the Chinese and then against them in a manner characteristic of the early travelers who saw the land with a more objective clarity than the later Jesuits. The general tone of the dialogue is favorable, however, particularly in its detailed accounts of the three sorts of examination provided for magistrates and the manner of their provincial government. The doctrine of Con-

---

[38]"An excellent treatise of the kingdome of China, and of the estate and government thereof: Printed in Latine at Macao a citie of the Portugals in China . . . ," Hakluyt, *Principal Navigations*, VI, 348–77.

[39]*Ibid.*, p. 353.

fucius is meted special praise: "The summe of the foresayd doctrine is, that men should follow the light of nature as their guide."[40] But the commentator tempers his praise:

All these things are in very deed praise-woorthy, if Confucius had made any mention of almighty God and of the life to come, and had not ascribed so much unto the heavens and unto fatall necessity, nor yet had so curiously entreated of worshipping the images of their forefathers.[41]

A similar detachment characterized Elizabethan references to China.[42] George Puttenham meeting with a gentleman in Italy "who had long travailed the Orientall parts of the world" obtained from him some curious insights into Chinese poetry,[43] but generally speaking, contemporary references to the Chinese language, their manner of printing, binding of feet, government, and religious beliefs were brief, stereotyped, and not overlaudatory. Writers of such encyclopedic mind as Francis Bacon[44] or Walter Raleigh[45] could hardly avoid mention of China in the course of their voluminous works, but no more than a tolerant interest characterized their thoughts on the subject. In his monument to melancholy Burton praised the "neat, polite, terse" people of China, their thrift, industry, good government, and civil service examinations, all of which he found admirable deterrents to the ravages of that disease.[46]

[40] *Ibid.*, p. 372.   [41] *Ibid.*, pp. 372–73.

[42] Ch'ien Chung-shu, "China in the English Literature of the Seventeenth Century," *Quarterly Bulletin of Chinese Bibliography*, I, No. 4 (December, 1940), 351–84; Robert R. Cawley, *Unpathed Waters*, Princeton, 1940.

[43] George Puttenham, *The Arte of English Poesie*, ed. Gladys Willcock and Alice Walker (Cambridge, 1936), pp. 91–94, 106–7. This is a reprint of the 1589 edition.

[44] Francis Bacon, *Opera Omnia* (London, 1730), I, 142, 159, 387; II, 137, 237; III, 69, 382.

[45] Sir Walter Raleigh, *The History of the World*, Book I, Ch. VII. In *Works* (Oxford, 1829), II, 222.

[46] Robert Burton, *The Anatomy of Melancholy*, ed. A. F. Bullen (London, 1923), I, 87, 102, 104–5, 115–16.

But their indiscriminate meat-eating, strong imagination, and the golden servitude (*aurea mancipia*) of their kings, he found sad incentives to melancholy.[47] Like the aforementioned authors, however, his interest was essentially transient.

The part which the greatest empire of the East played in the vast tracts of Elizabethan drama is even less consequential.[48] The plays harbor no Chinese characters or scenes. Playwrights, when they considered China at all, apparently felt for it an amused contempt inspired by the narratives of such men as Pinto and Mendoza who peered at wonders "through multiplying glasses."[49] It was diverting for the Tudor Londoner to read tall tales of the *Admiranda Pequini*—24,000 bargemen and 100,000 launderers—and in the mouths of Shakespeare's characters a "Cataian" became synonymous with a diverting Munchausen.[50]

Generally speaking, in this literature China was no more than a small piece in the mosaic of the rapidly ever-expanding universe. Beyond an enthusiasm for its commercial prospects and solid government, it enjoyed no perceptible vogue in Elizabethan and early Stuart England. The accounts of the merchantmen and missionaries were not yet heavily weighted in the Chinese favor. But by the mid-seventeenth century the trend had altered. Under Jesuit auspices the hardheaded approach of most of the merchantmen was gradually supplanted. Locked in a bitter quarrel with the Dominicans over the means of converting China, the Jesuits steeped themselves in Chinese culture and sought to assimilate it into Catholic doctrine. They sought to justify this extreme, if not heretical, indirection, by praising to the skies the civilization of their

[47]*Ibid.*, I, 249, 265, 304, 419–20; II, 173, 199.

[48]Robert R. Cawley, *The Voyagers and Elizabethan Drama* (Boston, 1938), pp. 208–31.

[49]James Howell, *Instructions for Forreine Travell* (London, 1869), p. 64. This is a reprint of the second edition of 1650.

[50]*Merry Wives of Windsor*, II, i, 148; *Twelfth Night*, II, iii, 77.

would-be converts. Unquestionably, as men of broad learning, many felt a deep and genuine sympathy with Chinese culture, and under their stimulus a new type of Sinological literature began to emerge.

As little by little the attitude toward China had shifted from a medieval one of wonder to one of realistic appraisal, so during the seventeenth century it was to alter again to one of calculated adulation. The rich and confused material of these accounts gave food for thought to many seventeenth century writers, in particular the theological polemicists. But when we examine their work we move into a different atmosphere. We move away from the vigorous narratives, away from the harsh glare of China seas and the tumult of alien lands to the seclusion and twilight of the study.

FATHER ADAM SCHALL, A JESUIT MISSIONARY
Kircher, 1670
From the collection of Avery Library

MAKOU (MACAO)
Nieuhoff, 1669

II

A CONFUSION OF
TONGUES

*T*HE SEVENTEENTH CENTURY SCHOLARS AND DIVINES delighted in dark imponderables, and the flames of the controversies they so enjoyed were fed continuously by the researches of antiquarians and the experiments of the new science. Besides these, the narratives of travelers over uncharted seas and lands kept the polemical fires at white heat. In the ensuing debates China's part was not altogether a minor one.[1]

To a great extent, however, early references to it pivot around a specific problem of Biblical interpretation. Tainted by incipient deism, hair-splitting scholars raked over the Scriptures to construct curious and ingenious exegeses. The interpretation of the confounding at Babel particularly appealed to them. They pondered the Genesis account of the sons of Noah who had settled on the plains of Shinar and attempted to build the tower to touch heaven. Up to this point scriptural history was clear. But God's judgment on these people was a more cryptic matter.

And the Lord said; Behold, the people *is* one, and they have all one language; and this they begin to do: and now nothing will be restrained from them, which they have imagined to do.

Go to, let us go down, and there confound their language, that they may not understand one another's speech.

So the Lord scattered them abroad from thence, upon the face of all the earth: and they left off to build the city.

[1]Ch'ien Chung-shu, "China in the English Literature of the Seventeenth Century," *Quarterly Bulletin of Chinese Bibliography*, I, No. 4 (December, 1940), 351–84, lists many references to China.

Therefore is the name of it called Babel; because the Lord did there confound the language of all the earth; and from thence did the Lord scatter them abroad upon the face of all the earth.[2]

Over these verses students of language and Biblical history divided, and in the speculations of both groups China had a place. Those more infected by skepticism dared to interpret the passage loosely to allow for the possible survival of the primitive tongue. The more rigidly orthodox insisted on a literal interpretation. Both groups deplored the problem of the multiplicity of tongues, but each proposed a different solution. The orthodox rebelled at the thought of seeking out a lost language. Why disturb the dust of centuries in heretical efforts to articulate fragments of the primitive tongue? Why not instead invent a new and perfected language? The idea was a recurrent hope in the intellectual world, and of particular appeal to both scholarly divines and more liberally minded scientists and philosophers.[3] Toward this end Athanasius Kircher had experimented hopefully with numbers.[4] Descartes and Leibniz were as keenly interested in reconciling divergences of languages,[5] and Bacon in his plans for the advancement of learning found himself constantly plagued by the ambiguities and defects of words. Though he accepted the confusion as a punishment on mankind,[6] he believed that God

[2]Genesis 11: 6–9.

[3]See Louis Couturat and Leopold Leau, *Histoire de la langue universelle*, Paris, 1903; Otto Funcke, *Zum Weltsprachen Problem in England im 17 Jahrhundert*, Heidelberg, 1929; Clark Emery, "John Wilkins' Universal Language," *Isis*, XXXVIII (February, 1948), 174–85; P. E. Stojan, *Bibliografio de internacio linguo*, Geneva, 1929.

[4]Athanasius Kircher, *Polygraphia nova et universalis, ex combinatoria arte detecta*, Rome, 1663.

[5]See Descartes's letter to Mersenne dated 20 November, 1629. Chapter III of Louis Couturat, *La Logique de Leibniz*, Paris, 1901, is devoted to Leibniz' interest in this project.

[6]Francis Bacon, *Opera Omnia* (London, 1730), I, 47 (*Instauratio Magna*, Part I), and III, 547 (*Of an Holy War*).

had at least not prohibited man from seeking to perfect an artificial language. Robert Boyle, to a great extent, shared his feelings. Writing to Samuel Hartlib, then engaged on *A Common Writing* (1647), he remarked: "If the design of the Real Character take effect, it will in good part make amends to mankind for what their pride lost them at the Tower of Babel."[7]

In the search for this universal language, Chinese character writing understandably received some attention. Hartlib's associate, John Durie, whose outlook was similarly cosmopolitan and who was likewise interested in a philosophical college of encyclopedic scope, recognized the necessity of synthesizing current linguistic knowledge and finding a means to "perfeit the knowledge of Oriental tongues."[8] But his enthusiasm was not shared by Cave Beck who in his *Universal Character* (1657), "Babel reversed,"[9] found no place in his system of numerals and letters for Chinese "scraules . . . which are such for their fashion that a European with his one Eye (which they afford him) would think they shut both theirs (they so much boast of) when they drew the shapes of those Characters."[10]

Lack of knowledge of Chinese characters handicapped these proponents of a universal language as much as its ideography appealed to them. It stimulated theorists because it suggested a calligraphy based on ideas rather than arbitrary sounds, and on this intellectual basis they thought a universal language might be developed. Bacon had contemplated with interest the Chinese "characteres quidam reales, non nominales, qui scilicet

[7]Letter of 19 March, 1646, quoted in Thomas Birch, *Life of Robert Boyle* (London, 1744), p. 73.

[8]Quoted on p. 12 of George H. Turnbull's *Samuel Hartlib*, London, 1919.

[9]Joseph Waite's "Prefatory Verses" to Cave Beck's *The Universal Character*, London, 1657.

[10]Cave Beck's Preface to *The Universal Character*.

nec literas, nec verba, sed res & notiones exprimunt."[11] Others had arrived at a similar notion independently. The irrepressible Sir Thomas Urquhart, momentarily laying aside his Adamitic genealogical charts, in his curious *Logopandecteision* (1653) had proposed a language in which each letter of each word would have a meaning, a project also suggested by the Marquis of Worcester.[12] Urquhart outlined sixty-six advantages of such a language, but after six preliminary books of fanfare he failed to unveil it. George Dalgarno, the developer if not the inventor of the deaf and dumb language, elaborated a similar but more serious thesis and divided all language into seventeen classes of ideas for which he used the letters of the Latin alphabet supplemented by two Greek characters.[13] John Wilkins, the bishop of Chester, in *An Essay toward a Real Character and a Philosophical Language* (1668), published seven years after Dalgarno's work, pushed this idea still further.[14] Nowhere did he acknowledge his predecessor's work but, as Horace Walpole facetiously suggested, these theories had perhaps been given impetus in other ways. Could not the good bishop's interest in flying have generated his interest in a universal language? In *The Discovery of a New World in the Moon* (1638) Wilkins had projected a fictional voyage to that planet. Obviously, as Walpole pointed out, a universal language would obviate the necessity of a lunar interpreter.[15] Whatever his inspiration, Wilkins weighed the possibility of adopting Chinese as the universal character. He was deterred, however, by the multiplicity of its ideograms, some 80,000,

[11]Bacon, *Opera Omnia*, I, 159 (*Instauratio Magna*, Book VI, ch. i).

[12]This project is discussed in John Willcock's *Sir Thomas Urquhart* (London, 1899), pp. 175 ff. See also the Marquis of Worcester's *Century of the Names . . .* , London, 1663, section 32.

[13]George Dalgarno, *Ars Signorum*, London, 1661.

[14]See Emery's, "John Wilkins' Universal Language," *Isis*, XXXVIII, 174–85.

[15]Horace Walpole, *Letters*, ed. Mrs. Paget Toynbee (Oxford, 1905), XIII, 199; Oct. 15, 1784, to Henry Conway.

which he feared would discourage the most conscientious of students, and, in addition, he found in analyzing a Chinese version of the Lord's Prayer that the analogy between the characters and the things they represented was at times difficult to fathom.[16]

Later proponents of the universal character paid little attention to Chinese. Sinological studies were too little advanced, and the difficulties of utilizing Chinese became increasingly apparent. But the cabal of scholars who thought the primitive language had not been confounded did not lose interest in China so quickly. The search for the lost language of Noah offered so fertile a field it was not easily exhausted.

Such a quest irresistibly appealed to that passionate antiquarian, Sir Thomas Browne. A mind that restlessly debated the songs the Sirens sang and the name Achilles assumed when he hid among the women could not long overlook such a temptation. In his *Essay on Languages and Particularly of the Saxon Tongue* he zestfully approached the problems of the permutations of language.[17] The mysteries of Babel suggested to him a host of joyous vexations. How, for example, had a universal language been maintained during the 1600 years between the creation and the flood? Would not "humorous inventions, necessities and new objects" have caused a Babel long before the confusion of tongues?[18] But even supposing that they had not, when the confusion fell at Shinar, what had become of those absent or those left behind at the original resting place of the ark? Had not the posterity of Noah dispersed before the migration to Shinar? In consequence, might not the primitive language have persisted unconfounded in some corners of the world?

[16]John Wilkins, *An Essay toward a Real Character and a Philosophical Language* (London, 1668), pp. 451–52.

[17]Sir Thomas Browne, *Works*, ed. Geoffrey Keynes (London, 1931), V, 83–98.

[18]*Ibid.*, p. 83.

These problems were heady draughts for Sir Thomas. One dark speculation led to another, and pondering over the Greek chronology developed in *De vera aetate mundi* by Isaac Vossius, one of the chief believers in China's primacy, Browne mused over the origin of those followers of Nimrod who had migrated from the east to Shinar. Like other scholars he found the Greek chronology clearly unable to account for the wide dispersal of humanity over the earth in the space of a mere 500 years. Consequently he consulted the records of other nations, among them the Chinese. In the *Commonplace Book* of his daughter, Elizabeth Lyttelton, we find, in his hand, this entry: "The books which my daughter Elizabeth hath read unto me at nights till she read them all out," followed by a formidable catalog which includes Semedo's *History of China*, all of the narratives of Fernam Mendez Pinto, and parts of Purchas.[19] During the long candle-lit evenings he mulled over these mountainous folios. Little by little the material sifted through his mind. Much as the subject appealed to him, nonetheless, in his final estimate of China's antiquity and language Browne remained characteristically ambivalent.

The Chinoys, who live at the bounds of the Earth, who have admitted little communication, and suffered successive incursions from one Nation, may possibly give account of a very ancient Language; but consisting of many Nations and Tongues; confusion, admixtion and corruption in the length of time might probably so have crept in as without the virtue of a common Character and lasting Letter of things, they could never probably make out those strange memorials which they pretend, while they still make use of the Works of their great Confutius many hundred years before Christ, and in a series ascend as high as Poncuus, who is conceived our Noah.[20]

[19]*Ibid.*, pp. 295–96.   [20]*Ibid.*, pp. 85–86.

Perhaps he sensed that in these cogitations lay the seeds of heresy. At all events, he preferred to leave such problems unsolved, refusing to surrender the delights of speculation for the certainty of dogma. His further observations on China are trifling and unimportant.

But the problem of the primitive language and its implications troubled scholars and churchmen for over a century. While Browne had approached it obliquely, others, less sensitive, rushed headlong into the controversy. They compared the views of rival historians. They examined in Raleigh the claims of the Armenians;[21] they weighed the arguments of Peter Heylyn in favor of the Hebrews.[22] But in the course of these recondite speculations, problems other than merely linguistic ones arose. It became necessary to appraise conflicting histories. The possessors of the primitive language had, of necessity, a high antiquity, and the study of ancient chronologies brought some troublesome discrepancies to light. The pagan annals disordered and confused the well-ordered outlines of Christian history, and a wealth of material for the skeptics was dredged up in the subsequent arguments.

Of these none is more curious than John Webb's *An Historical Essay Endeavoring a Probability That the Language of the Empire of China Is the Primitive Language* (1669).[23] If he is all but forgotten now, the author was known in his own day as the assistant of Inigo Jones, as a fervent royalist, and an antiquarian who delighted in the mysteries of Stonehenge. In this vigorous essay, lent an air of scientific validity by its publication at Gresham College, Webb voiced still another enthusiasm. Never a philological scholar (his closest

[21]Sir Walter Raleigh, *The History of the World,* Book I, Ch. VII. *Works* (Oxford, 1829), II, 218 ff.

[22]Peter Heylyn, *Cosmography,* 5th ed. (London, 1677), p. 7.

[23]Cordier lists a second edition of this work as appearing in 1678. This edition, Cordier states, is a reissue of the 1669 edition with a new title page.

approach to this was his design for the frontispiece to Brian
Walton's 1657 Polyglot Bible), his account of the splendors
and antiquities of China not only complicated linguistic
questions but hopelessly entangled Biblical-historical problems
as well.[24]

The *Historical Essay* was dedicated to Charles I in terms
which must have puzzled that august monarch, and opened
with a thesis as simple as it was bold. On the assumption that
the Chinese language had petrified, and that consequently its
characters had remained virtually unaltered, Webb set out to
prove, by ransacking Scripture and history, that China had been
peopled while the earth still spoke one language; hence
theirs was the primitive tongue. He invoked d'Espagne and
Crinesius to corroborate him on the persistence of the primitive
tongue from the time of Adam to Noah,[25] and on this shaky
assumption set about to prove the descent of the Chinese from
Noah. To do so it was necessary to answer a vital question.
Where was Ararat on which Noah's ark had landed? With
the devotion of a fanatic he raked over ancient and modern
biographers and historians for the answer. His meditation over
Raleigh and Becanus led him to a triumphant conclusion. Noah
had settled in India. This solution arrived at, still another
question presented itself. What had become of his progeny?
Weighing Kircher's account of Noah and his children against
that of the cosmographer Heylyn, Webb wholeheartedly endorsed the latter's claim that the posterity of Shem had peopled
China.[26] The contention was not, after all, a surprising one.
Had not Semedo, Vossius, and Martin Martinius all attested

[24]See Ch'en Shou-yi, "John Webb, a Forgotten Page in the Early History
of Sinology in Europe," *Chinese Social and Political Science Review*, XIX,
No. 3 (October, 1935), 295–330.
[25]John Webb, *An Historical Essay Endeavoring a Probability That the
Language of the Empire of China Is the Primitive Language* (London,
1669), p. 17.
[26]Heylyn, *Cosmography*, pp. 7 ff.

to the antiquity of China and her possession of letters before the rest of Asia, if not the rest of the world?[27]

Grotesque as such genealogical reckoning may seem, Webb had considerable backing for it. Imaginative early narratives, Elizabethan travel books, and seventeenth century geographies swarm with such notions. John De Marignolli's *Recollections of Eastern Travel* had confronted Biblical historical problems with like assurance. It had demonstrated infallibly that Shem was given dominion over the Far East and that Adam's footprint and house were still visiblē in Ceylon.[28] Nathaniel Carpenter's *Geographie Delineated* (1625) had confidently located Ararat between Scythia and India.[29] Peter Heylyn's popular *Cosmography* (1652) was merely repeating a well-worn contention in suggesting that China had been peopled by the posterity of Noah before Babel.[30] These were actualities, Webb seemed to believe, established almost beyond doubt. He found, of course, minor points of disagreement with his sources. Heylyn had fallen into the unfortunate error of believing Hebrew to be the primitive language, but such theories, patently absurd in the light of fact, Webb dismissed along with similar nonsense to the effect that Adam spoke Dutch in Paradise.

After satisfying himself as to the direct Adamitic descent of the Chinese and the untarnished purity of their language, he centered his argument on an effort to harmonize Biblical and Chinese chronology. Ferreting out suggestions and hypotheses to effect this reconciliation, he pyramided one supposition on

[27]F. Alvarez Semedo, *The History of That Great and Renowned Monarchy of China* (London, 1655), p. 31; Isaac Vossius, *Dissertatio de vera aetate mundi* (The Hague, 1659), p. 44; Martin Martinius, *Novus Atlas Sinensis* (Amsterdam, 1655), p. 1.

[28]See Sir Henry Yule, *Cathay and the Way Thither* (London, 1914), III, 197, 246–47.

[29]Nathaniel Carpenter, *Geographie Delineated*, 2d ed. (London, 1635), p. 213.

[30]Heylyn, *Cosmography*, p. 187 (*Lib. III*).

another. In doing so, he differed little from later scholars who sought to integrate the remote civilizations of the Americas into the orthodox patterns of Biblical history, but Webb pushed his arguments to still more ludicrous lengths. Seizing upon a reference in Chinese annals to a deluge, he proposed that the flood in the time of the Emperor Jaus (Yao) was the universal one. Could not Noah therefore have been a resident of China? It was not beyond probability. Had not Sir Thomas Browne referred to the possibility that Noah and Poncuus (Pan Ku) were one? Was it not even more likely that Noah and the Emperor Jaus were identical? Both were just and upright husbandmen and preachers; both had suffered from the ravages of a flood and from the crimes of a wicked son. The identification seemed almost inescapable.[31] Such were the flimsy foundations of argument on which Webb raised a staggering superstructure of speculation.

In praising the Chinese, however, he sedulously courted orthodoxy and shunned the chronological pitfalls of his source, Martinius's *Sinicae historiae decas prima,* based on the Chinese dynastic histories. Webb was intent upon proving the Chinese the inheritors not only of the language of Noah, but also of his religion. Like the Jesuits he rejoiced in correspondences between Chinese religious beliefs and Christianity, such as their use of the word "Shang-ti" to denote the supreme governor of heaven and earth.[32] Confucius, "the Plato of the Chinois," he apostrophized not as the atheistic apostle of natural morality, as the deists later hailed him, but as the prophet of the Word made Flesh and the coming of the Savior in the West. Unlike the deists also, Webb denied that the Chinese were slaves to a religion of pure reason. He found instead that

[31] Webb, *An Essay Endeavoring a Probability,* pp. 60–62.

[32] The Rites Controversy and the part which this word played in it are splendidly discussed in Arnold W. Rowbotham's *Missionary and Mandarin* (Berkeley, 1942), Chs. IX–XII.

they had always "most avoided to be guided by the light of Nature, and least erred in the rules of their Religion."[33]

All in all, his attitude savored of the paradoxical orthodoxy of the Jesuits. The extravagance of his praises of China foreshadowed the paeans of the deists, though the latter sought to intensify the clash between the Christian and Chinese chronologies and to exalt the natural morality of the Confucians at the expense of Christianity. The chief value of Webb's book lay in his effort to fit China into a cosmological pattern. In this respect he anticipated the efforts of eighteenth century Orientalists to interrelate Egyptian hieroglyphics and Chinese characters and to assess their contributions to the culture of Greece and the New World. The drawbacks of Webb's book were many. His historical interpretations were not bolstered by fact. His discussion of language was rudimentary, for he based it on the assumption that Kuan-hua was the primitive tongue, and he avoided examination of the many Chinese dialects.[34] His philosophical displays were limited to explaining the corruption of some Chinese words and to formulating a list of six requisites for a primitive language, all of which he found, hardly to his own surprise, satisfied in Chinese. Nevertheless, grotesque as it was in conception and logic, his work exposed the deepening implications of the problem of China's place in the sun.

Few as the indications are that his book was widely read, it was at least well known to one of his contemporaries, Sir Matthew Hale, who read *An Historical Essay* with interest, even if he found himself in disagreement with it on almost every point. In *The Primitive Origination of Mankind Considered and Examined According to the Light of Nature* (1677), Hale took a righteously orthodox stand. He examined closely

---

[33]Webb, *An Essay Endeavoring a Probability*, p. 86.

[34]This is discussed at length in Ch'en Shou-yi's "John Webb," *Chinese Social and Political Science Review*, XIX, 295–330.

Webb's theory that the ark had landed in the mountains which surround China and that the Western Continent might have been peopled from there, but Webb's contention that Moses had written only for the Israelites, and had therefore omitted much historical fact, displeased Hale who accepted Moses as the most reliable of historians. Allured by the annals of Egypt and China, he nonetheless scented their dangerous inferences and condemned them as legendary, preferring to interpret literally the confounding of tongues, and, despite Webb's arguments, finding the identity of the primitive language indiscernible.

Such problems, linguistic and historical, were obviously still far from solution. When that august body, The Royal Society, turned their attention to them, Robert Hook touched briefly upon these troublesome points.[35] In his discussion of Chinese characters he reported without comment the Chinese claim that Fohi (Fu Hsi), the inventor of characters, had lived 2950 years before Christ. He studied the language as best he could, but the conclusions left him dubious. "I fear the Relations I have hitherto met with concerning it, were written by such as did not well understand it,"[36] he comments sadly, an observation which few would dispute. Further study led him to the inescapable conclusion: "I conceive the present *Chinese* Language to have no affinity with the Character, the true primitive, or first Language, or pronunciation of it, having been lost."[37]

The Royal Society's pronunciamento did not, however, spell an end to the controversy. The dangerously heretical search for the primitive language persisted into the eighteenth century. The flames continued to flicker intermittently. On men of great learning but precarious intellectual balance the subject

[35]Robert Hook, "Some Observations and Conjectures Concerning Chinese Characters," *Philosophical Transactions of the Royal Society*, XVI (March–April, 1686), 63–78.

[36]*Ibid.*, p. 69.   [37]*Ibid.*, p. 73.

still exercised an irresistible appeal. Articulating complex cosmologies, such men as William Whiston wrestled anew with the problem.[38] From one edition to another of Whiston's popular work his conclusions altered.[39] In his *New Theory of the Earth* (1696) he tentatively accepted the thesis that the Occidentals were the offspring of Shem, Ham, and Japhet, and China peopled by the descendants of Noah. How, otherwise, could one account for its large population, since the dispersal from Babel had been so slow? How else could one account for the superior Chinese government and learning, save as a product of the superior wisdom of Noah? Like Webb, Whiston inclined strongly to the belief that Noah and Fohi were identical;[40] and he accepted the theory of the universal deluge to the extent of assigning the inundation of Peking to Friday, November 28, 2365 B.C. at high noon.[41] (His assurance in this matter gave confidence to the Duchess of Bolton who confided to the amused Walpole that she intended to escape an imminent worldwide conflagration by fleeing to China.[42] Presumably she hoped to encounter a resourceful descendant of Noah-Fohi.) But Whiston's assurance wavered in the later editions of his work, and in them China's place in world history was far more tentatively sketched.

Deep into the eighteenth century, however, scholars continued to follow false fires. In his *Sacred and Profane History of the World* (1731-37) Samuel Shuckford echoed his predecessors.

There is indeed another language in the world, which seems to have some marks of its being the original language of mankind,

[38]William Whiston, *A New Theory of the Earth* . . . , London, 1696.
[39]The permutations in Whiston's work are well discussed in Katherine Collier's *Cosmogonies of Our Fathers,* New York, 1934.
[40]Whiston, *A New Theory of the Earth,* 2d ed. (London, 1708), p. 140.
[41]*Ibid.,* p. 381.
[42]Walpole, *Letters,* II, 124; Aug. 1, 1745, to George Montagu.

namely, the Chinese. . . . Noah, as has been observed, very probably settled in these parts; and if the great father and restorer of mankind came out of the ark and settled here, it is very probable that he left here the one universal language of the world.[43]

The suggestion was tendered warily, however, and Shuckford, like Browne, refused to commit himself on this issue. Too many had found their search a sleeveless errand. The primitive tongue had not been established, nor had the cause for divergences in language. Neither those who defended the miracle of Babel nor those who discounted it could present a wholly satisfactory argument. The subject had provided little more than an occasion for display of ingenuity.

Other polemicists such as William Wotton sensed, moreover, the heresies such controversy had bred. By the time Wotton was at work on his posthumously published *Discourse Concerning the Confusion of Languages at Babel* (1732), the poisonous outcroppings were already painfully evident.[44] In this essay, written at the end of a lifetime filled with disappointments, he summoned all the resources of his scholarship to crush the persistent disbelievers who refused to credit the miraculous confounding. To ground his arguments unshakably he embarked upon a comparative analysis of the Eastern and Western languages to prove the impossibility that all had developed from one tongue. But the immensity of the project discouraged even one who had studied Latin and Greek at five and Hebrew at six. He was troubled with the tiresome queries of such men as Reland and Stiernhielmius who asked, among other things, why God, if He wished to punish man, had not widely separated those whose language was similar. Wearily he fell back on the explanation that God did not

---

[43]Samuel Shuckford, *Sacred and Profane History of the World*, 4th ed. (London, 1808), I, 106.

[44]William Wotton, *A Discourse Concerning the Confusion of Languages at Babel* (London, 1732), pp. 43 ff.

want to punish them too much. But ultimately even he was forced to reiterate the unscholarly but inevitable conclusion—the variety of languages was unaccountable, the oldest language impossible of determination, and the world in all probability not older than the Mosaic account.

The quarrel, fitfully resurrected, dragged its slow length through the eighteenth century, and as late as 1760 Goldsmith felt the Noah-Fohi controversy still fresh enough to satirize.[45] The reasons for its persistent outbreaks are not far to seek.

Perhaps the primary reason was the lack of real scholarship in Oriental languages. Thomas Hyde, the Orientalist and Persian scholar, enthusiastic as he was for things Chinese, had little knowledge of the language beyond what he had picked up from Shen Fo Tsung, Father Couplet's protégé, who visited England in 1685.[46] While Chinese characters had been printed in a European book (Mendoza's *Historia*) as early as 1585, and later in Golius' *De regno Catayo additamentum* and Kircher's *China illustrata* (1667) they remained enigmas to virtually the entire learned world of Europe. The Bodleian, though it boasted a collection of Chinese books, the gifts of English nobles and merchantmen, had no readers to take advantage of them.[47] The confusion which typifies Hook's account of Chinese characters is hardly less evident in the controversy a century later over the inscription on the Turin bust.[48] It was not until the nineteenth century that England was to produce really great scholars of Chinese.

In the second place, the problems of chronology involved in the debate over Babel were for a long period insoluble. Only in the latter part of the eighteenth century did rudimentary

[45]Oliver Goldsmith, *A Citizen of the World*, Letter 89.

[46]See Chapter VII. Also Thomas Hyde, "Praefatio ad Lectorem," in *Mandragorias seu Historia Shahiludi*, Oxford, 1694.

[47]William D. Macray, *Annals of the Bodleian Library*, 2d ed. (Oxford, 1890), pp. 86–88, 128, 154, 167, 422 (footnote).

[48]See Chapter VIII.

comparative studies in history and culture begin to integrate the materials of the seventeenth century cosmologies on broader and sounder bases.

But in the final analysis the prolongation of the effort to prove the Chinese the possessors of the primitive tongue has an emotional basis. On men of sensitively keyed imagination the mysteries of China exercised a continuing fascination. As late as the nineteenth century its unfathomable antiquity evoked a reluctant reverence in one of its bitterest critics. In describing the monstrous Oriental scenes and apparitions of his opium dreams, De Quincey made at the same time perhaps the most logical *apologia* for the quarrelsome pedants of the seventeenth century:

Southern Asia, in general, is the seat of awful images and associations. As the cradle of the human race it would alone have a dim and reverential feeling connected with it. . . . The mere antiquity of Asiatic things, of their institutions, histories, modes of faith, *etc.*, is so impressive, that to me the vast age of the race and name overpowers the sense of the individual. A young Chinese seems to me an antediluvian man renewed.[49]

[49]Thomas De Quincey, *Confessions of an English Opium-Eater,* entry for May, 1818.

III

CONFUCIUS, THE
GOOD GOVERNOR

*T*HE BABEL CONTROVERSY was long a-dying, but while the reverberations of the dispute were slowly attenuated some opinions on China became generally accepted. Missionaries and travelers alike, from the sixteenth century on, in addition to noting such curiosities as the Great Wall, the manufacture of porcelain, and cormorant fishing, concurred in their praise of China's peaceful and stable government.[1] By 1660 its reputation in this respect was established. In the decades that followed, China also became renowned for superior morality, and in the person of Confucius these two merits were fused.[2] Under the stimulus of Jesuit narratives and translations, and the enthusiasm of various essayists and philosophers, the cult of the sage began.

"Sancte Confuci, ora pro nobis!" La Mothe le Vayer exclaimed in a moment of exaltation.[3] He was not alone in his fervor, for the sage represented to many the good governor and enlightened moralist. Though the voyagers of the sixteenth and early seventeenth centuries had stressed the order and tranquillity that prevailed in Canton and Amoy, a contrast perhaps to the tension of Elizabeth's England and the turmoil of Philip the Second's Iberian empire, they did not clearly re-

[1]Ch'ien Chung-shu, "China in the English Literature of the Seventeenth Century," *Quarterly Bulletin of Chinese Bibliography*, I, No. 4 (1940), 351–84; Tsen-Chung Fan, "Chinese Culture in England from Sir William Temple to Oliver Goldsmith," *Harvard University Summaries of Ph.D. Theses 1931*, pp. 223–26.

[2]Arnold H. Rowbotham, "The Impact of Confucianism on Seventeenth Century Europe," *Far Eastern Quarterly*, IV, No. 3 (May, 1945), 224–42.

[3]*Journal des Scavants*, Amsterdam, 7 June, 1688, p. 39.

late this to the morality of its governors. However, as the missionaries arrived in increasing numbers and sought to orient themselves for a more lasting stay, they were forced to appraise the nature of this government more carefully. The China they found, despite its recent conquest by the Manchus, was administered by a scholar-class steeped in Confucian traditions. Anxious to consolidate their rule, the usurpers had shrewdly enlisted the support of the most conservative element of the empire, and under K'ang Hsi Confucian studies were rigorously pursued. It was a policy that played into the hands of the Jesuits.

By 1687 when Père le Comte and the French missionary group reached Macao, the Jesuit position had become extremely precarious, both theologically and diplomatically. Franciscans and Dominicans, angered at the latitudinarianism of the Jesuits and their high positions of trust in the imperial courts, had already brought grave charges against them. They quarreled with the Jesuit contention that the Confucian rites in honor of the sage and the ceremonies at ancestral shrines had no more than a social and political significance, and they attacked the Jesuit interpretation of "Shang-ti" as a reference to a Supreme Being. The missionaries were forced therefore to steer a perilous middle course between the See of Rome and the Dragon Throne.[4] They could not deny the sage and his rites. Neither could they exalt them. Their policy depended on relating his teachings as closely as possible to those of Christianity. Consequently they stressed the fragmentary Chinese knowledge of a Virgin-born savior and acclaimed Confucius, as the scholastics had Plato, as a prophet of a Savior from the West and as a teacher whose sayings closely paralleled those of the Redeemer.

[4] Arnold H. Rowbotham, *Missionary and Mandarin* (Berkeley, 1942), Chs. IX–XII. See also Kenneth S. Latourette, *A History of Christian Missions in China*, New York, 1929, and Antonio S. Rosso, *Apostolic Legations to China of the Eighteenth Century*, 1948.

In doing so they were forced to suppress other aspects of
Chinese religious thought. In Buddhism they found a disturb-
ing inversion of the Catholic ritual, an alarming parody of the
Mass complicated by the basest superstitions.[5] In Taoism they
found a decadent cult of alchemy and magic, pledged to distill
the elixir of immortality. Under such trappings it was difficult
to detect the noble pagan. The Confucian, on the other hand,
handicapped though he was by seeing Christianity through a
glass darkly, was a far more tolerable figure. He was relatively
easier to assimilate into the European world where, under Jesuit auspices, he became so noted a figure that until the late
eighteenth century he almost completely eclipsed Buddha and
Lao-Tse and became, indeed, almost synonymous with Chinese culture.

The earliest accounts of the travelers and missionaries had
laid the groundwork for the eulogies of this man "of most upright and incorrupt manners."[6] Ricci and Trigault had praised
him as the prince of philosophers, the peer, if not the superior,
of the noble pagans of Greece and Rome, and the spiritual
leader of China's scholar-governors: "The scope of this Liter-
ate sect is, the peace and good of the Commonwealth, and of
Families, and of each person."[7] Father Intorcetta in 1667 published a life of the sage, and Semedo, Athanasius Kircher, and
many others had made the name a familiar and reverenced
one.

Such a figure fitted admirably into the European philosphi-
cal background. In France as early as 1642 La Mothe le Vayer

[5]"The Jesuits in the Far East," in Samuel Purchas, *Hakluytus Posthumus*
(Glasgow, 1906), XII, 281; Peter Heylyn, *Cosmography,* 5th ed. (London,
1677), p. 183. The account of China's religions in Louis Le Comte, *Memoirs and Observations . . .* , 3d ed. (London, 1699), pp. 309 ff., is characteristic.

[6]Anonymous, "An excellent Treatise of the Kingdome of China," in
Richard Hakluyt, *Principal Navigations* (Glasgow, 1904), VI, 372.

[7]Ricius and Trigautius, "A Discourse of the Kingdome of China," Purchas, *Hakluytus Posthumus,* XII, 459.

in his *Vertu des payens* had refused to consign Plato, Socrates, and Confucius to the perpetual fires.[8] In England such later works as Dryden's *Religio Laici* showed how favorable the philosophical climate was for a tolerant reception of the sage.[9] The Horatian *via media* of the well-tempered classicists was certainly not far removed from the Confucian Doctrine of the Mean.[10] Noting this receptiveness, the missionaries, in their anxiety to justify themselves, flooded Europe with translations of the Chinese classics and the writings of the sage. In *Sapientia Sinica* (1662) they introduced the *Ta Hsueh* (Great Learning) and *Lun Yü* (Analects) of Confucius to the Western world. Adding his *Chung Yung* (Doctrine of the Mean) to these earlier translations, and including also his biography and a chronology of China since 2697 B.C., they dedicated the ensuing composite, *Confucius Sinarum Philosophus* (1687), to no less a figure than Louis XIV.[11]

The publication of these translations proved as stimulating to the Europeans as the Jesuits had hoped. In France they provoked such tributes as *La Morale de Confucius, philosophe de la Chine* (1687) and Simon Fourcher's *Lettre sur la morale de Confucius* (1688), though they drew attacks as well from such men as Fenelon.[12] In Germany the translations also attracted much notice. They inflamed Christian Wolff to so passionate a stand on Chinese morality that it led to his dismissal

[8]Arnold H. Rowbotham, "La Mothe le Vayer's *Vertu des payens* and Eighteenth Century Cosmopolitanism," *Modern Language Notes,* LIII, No. 1 (January 1938), 10–14.

[9]Preface to *Religio Laici,* London, 1682.

[10]See Arthur O. Lovejoy, "The Parallel of Deism and Classicism," *Modern Philology,* XXIX (February, 1932), 281–99.

[11]In 1711 *Confucius Sinarum Philosophus* was reprinted in Prague by Father Noel with some additional material, including the book of Mencius.

[12]Adolf Reichwein, *China and Europe* (New York, 1925), pp. 75–98, discusses Confucius and the Enlightenment. Fenelon's dialogue between Socrates and Confucius in the *Dialogues des morts* was published posthumously.

from the University at Halle. They produced Leibniz' *Novissima Sinica* (1697) and his proposal of a universal system of natural theology.[13] In the book of *I-Ching* (Changes) he found the key to a world-wide system of natural ethics to replace formal dogma, and using the technique of the Jesuit Figurists he attempted to identify its reputed author, Fohi (Fu Hsi), with Hermes Trismegistus and perhaps Zoroaster and Enoch. Such results were in part gratifying, but the Jesuits found to their dismay that they had placed dangerous weapons in the hands of the enemies of the church.

In England, as well, the Confucian legend appealed to both orthodox and heterodox thinkers. Its materialism appealed to the English deists; the humanism and benevolent patriarchy endorsed by Confucius, and the perfected, if mummified, Chinese way of life gratified solid Tories and cautious Whigs. Confucius was the supreme apostle of the orderly *status quo*. It was the temper of the Augustans to find their Elysium not, as their descendants did, in the primitive innocence of the South Seas, but in the glories of a civilized past. With their instinctive Hobbesian distrust of a disorganized society, the classicists, both French and English, preferred the sage to the savage, the static to the dynamic. *The Morals of Confucius* (1691), as interpreted by Father Couplet, in most respects left unruffled the most die-hard principles of the Roi Soleil and the Stuarts.

Poverty and Human Miseries are Evils in themselves, but the wicked only resent them. 'Tis a Burden under which they groan, and which makes them at last to sink; they even distaste the best Fortune. 'Tis the Wise-Man only who is always pleas'd: Virtue renders his spirit quiet: Nothing troubles him, nothing disquiets

[13]Leibniz's interest in China is discussed in Ch. III of Louis Couturat's *La Logique de Leibniz*, Paris, 1901. See also Franz R. Merkel, *G. W. von Leibniz und die China-Mission*, Leipzig, 1920, and Donald F. Lach, "Leibniz and China," *Journal of the History of Ideas*, VI, No. 4 (October, 1945), 436–55.

him, because he practices not Virtue for a Reward. The practice of
Virtue is the sole Recompense he expects.[14]

It is very difficult to associate with the Populace. These sort of men
grow familiar and insolent when we have too much correspondence with them: And because they imagine they are slighted,
when never so little neglected, we draw their Aversion upon us.[15]

The more philosophical maxims were scarcely more disturb-
ing to the orthodox. The Preface to the *Morals* made the conventional assertion that the Chinese were not idolaters and
paid adoration only to the Creator of the Universe, and the
translators' choice of sayings was largely guided by the desire
to point as nice a parallel as possible between the maxims of
Confucius and those of the Christian church. A number, however, such as "The Natural Light is only a perpetual Conformity of our Soul with the Laws of Heaven,"[16] appealed to
more liberal thinkers.

It is not difficult to see why such material attracted the attention of Sir William Temple, the most fulsome English admirer of China. Though John Webb had attempted to spark
English interest earlier, Temple's enthusiasm for China and
Confucius was of a more persuasive and contagious kind. His
opinions were the distillation of a naturally cool scholarly
mind, and his judgment of the Chinese merits was tempered
by a lifetime of participation in public affairs.

Perhaps as early as 1654 he had turned his attention to the
subject when Dorothy Osborne, lamenting the tedious winter
days at Chicksands, wrote him of her pleasure in Fernam
Mendez Pinto's highly-colored *Story of China*.[17] Certainly before the end of his stay at The Hague in 1669 he had carefully
studied John Nieuhoff's *The Embassy of the Dutch East India*

[14]*The Morals of Confucius* (London, 1691), p. 119.
[15]*Ibid.*, p. 138.   [16]*Ibid.*, p. 139.
[17]*Letters of Dorothy Osborne to William Temple*, ed. G. C. Moore-Smith
(Oxford, 1928), p. 148.

Company to the Tartar Cham (1669) and in the twenty-year interim before the appearance of his essay *Of Heroic Virtue* (1690) he had read considerably more on the subject. Nieuhoff remained his main source of information, despite his further rumination over the accounts of Marco Polo, Martin Martinius, Athanasius Kircher, Magalhaens, and Montanus.[18] The allure of the subject must indeed have been magnetic to induce him to sift these mountains of material. But to a man of his cosmopolitan and skeptical intellect, such an appeal is understandable. China offered the spectacle of a great hierarchically disposed empire that satisfied him as a practical statesman. Its veneration for antiquity and tradition complemented his own preference for the civilization of Greece and Rome. Above all, the Confucian temper appealed strongly to his skeptical mind. So strong, in fact, was this appeal, that it provoked Bishop Burnet's darkest suspicions: "He was a great admirer of the sect of Confucius in China, who were atheists themselves, but left religion to the rabble."[19]

Though Temple in his writings touched upon many aspects of Chinese culture and history, his main concern was with the cult of this sage. Primarily, he admired Confucius because, like Socrates, he had turned men away from dizzy metaphysical speculation to the contemplation of a practical social morality of universal applicability. In his essay *Of Heroic Virtue* Temple's admiration achieved its fullest expression.

With the synthetic mind of a world historian, he focused his attention on four little-known countries—China, Peru, Scythia, and Arabia—and their manifestations of qualities arising "from some great and native excellency of temper or genius, transcending the common race of mankind in wisdom, goodness

[18]Clara Marburg, *Sir William Temple: a Seventeenth Century Libertin* (New Haven, 1932), 50–60, 108; Homer E. Woodbridge, *Sir William Temple, The Man and His Work* (New York, 1940), pp. 276–84.

[19]Bishop Gilbert Burnet, *The History of His Own Time* (London, 1724–34), I, 378.

and fortitude"[20]—a definition remarkably similar to Carlyle's conception of heroism. Scornful as he was of travel literature, nevertheless he prefaced his consideration of China with a leisurely consideration of its relations with the West, its geography and recent history, its chronology, and the heroic virtues of the emperor Fohi. All of these he subordinated, however, to his central interest—current Chinese virtues, political and moral, and, above all, the source of these virtues: Confucius, who had taught men to live well and govern well.

The sum of his writings seem to be a body or digestion of ethics, that is, of all moral virtues, either personal, economical, civil or political; and framed for the institution and conduct of men's lives, their families, and their governments, but chiefly of the last: the bent of his thoughts and reasonings running up and down this scale, that no people can be happy but under good governments, and no governments happy but over good men; and that for the felicity of mankind, all men in a nation, from the Prince to the meanest peasant, should endeavor to be good, and wise, and virtuous, as far as his own thoughts, the precepts of others, or the laws of his country can instruct him.[21]

In praising this gregarious and materialistic code of ethics which measured man's morality largely in terms of social progress, the skeptical Temple found himself in agreement with such staunch Catholics as Father Intorcetta who, in the *Sinarum Scientia Politico-Moralis* (Goa, 1669), with its appended life of Confucius, laid the same stress on the humanitarianism of the sage and its beneficial results. His morality, after all, had brought about something close to an earthly paradise—government by the intellectually elect, who were chosen through a rigid system of competitive examinations and were subject to constant critical scrutiny while in office.

[20]Sir William Temple, *Works* (London, 1814), III, 313.
[21]*Ibid.*, pp. 332–33.

Upon these foundations and institutions, by such methods and orders, the kingdom of China seems to be framed and policed with the utmost force and reach of human wisdom, reason and contrivance; and in practice to excel the very speculations of other men, and all those imaginary schemes of the European wits, the institutions of Xenophon, the republic of Plato, the Utopias, or Oceanas, of our modern writers.[22]

It was futile to trust to visionary Utopias, "witty fictions, but mere Chimeras," as Burton called them.[23] As Peter Heylyn observed in his Cosmography, China was a pleasing example of the realization of some of More's schemes.[24] Temple also was more concerned with concrete achievements than with ideal visions, and in a moral-political development such as the followers of Confucius had achieved he found the hope of mankind. Fatally subject though earthly kingdoms were to alteration and decay, an empire founded on such principles might well rise above the ruins of time.

While Temple found other displays of heroic virtue among the great men of Peru, Scythia, and Arabia, his praise of them was far more temperate. He lauded the virtues of Mahomet, but branded the Alcoran "a wild fanatic rhapsody of his visions or dreams,"[25] a far cry from the order and clarity of Confucius' maxims. In the final analysis he acclaimed the Chinese sage and his followers as the wisest of people and turned an approving eye on the four maxims of their benevolent patriarchic rule: the avoidance of innovation; the necessity of putting national and not private interests first; the encouragement of industry and thrift; and last of all, the prevention of dangers

---

[22]Ibid., p. 342. This passage was incorporated verbatim into The Tea-Table, No. 33, 1724, as quoted in B. Sprague Allen, Tides in English Taste (Cambridge, Mass., 1937), I, 184.

[23]Robert Burton, Anatomy of Melancholy, ed. A. F. Bullen (London, 1923), I, 113.

[24]Heylyn, Cosmography, p. 184.   [25]Temple, Works, III, 382.

from abroad.[26] Further principles of Confucian statesmanship doubtless suggested to him such specific remedies to better the English government as that no peer be allowed a voice in the government before the age of thirty, and that no officeholder enjoy more than one civil or military appointment simultaneously.[27]

Though Temple touched on other aspects of China (the asymmetrical "sharawadgi"[28] and the medical knowledge of the pulse),[29] these are subsidiary references. His interest remained centered on Confucius, whose genius had been directed toward so practical an aim—government by the intellectually and morally elect. The Chinese sage played only a small part in the *Essay on Ancient and Modern Learning;* nevertheless, Temple clearly enrolled him among the heroes of antiquity. Not polemic by design, the essay which precipitated the Battle of the Books was, however, far more than a retired statesman's graceful expression of a partiality for the culture of Rome and Greece.[30] Unwittingly, perhaps, Temple was voicing a theory of history as well. His urbanity and experience as a man of affairs led him to distrust the easy optimism and confident vision of the scientists of Gresham College. The rise and fall of empires and the broad vistas of world history inspired him with the gravest doubts of the triumphal march of the arts and sciences. History was not progress onward and upward. Rather, it seemed to him, a tempestuous cyclic flux, in which heroic virtue periodically rose from its own ashes. No matter how often time obliterated the achievements of the great, new heroes sprang up to reduplicate their triumphs. Knowledge was

[26]*Ibid.,* pp. 44–45, "Of Popular Discontents."

[27]*Ibid.,* pp. 55, 62.

[28]*Ibid.,* pp. 237–38, "Of Gardening." See also Chapter VI, below.

[29]Temple, *Works,* III, 297, "Of Health and Long Life."

[30]H. W. Garrod, "Phalaris and Phalarism," in *Seventeenth Century Studies: Presented to Sir Herbert Grierson* (Oxford, 1938), pp. 360–71.

largely a matter of rediscovery. As Greek learning had in large part derived from Egypt and Phoenicia, so, in all probability, the natural and moral philosophy of Pythagoras, Democritus, and Lycurgus had derived from India and China.[31] Where more naturally could the Greeks have found the doctrine of the transmigration of souls and the emphasis on the four cardinal virtues? Plagues, invasions, and the turns of empire might level civilizations and erase cultural debts, but was the proof extant that "the productions of Gresham College, or the late academies of Paris, outshined or eclipsed the Lycaeum of Plato, the academy of Aristotle, the Stoa of Zeno, the garden of Epicurus?"[32] Had not the same perfection been achieved perhaps in Chinese civilization? Such a belief in a finite body of knowledge would not have been displeasing to the most solid Confucian.

Temple's paeans to the Chinese and the sage did not, however, touch off a wave of enthusiasm. The English do not easily succumb to heroes and hero worship. Confucius might well be pleasing to the liberal philosophers of France and Germany, but John Bull did not take readily to rhapsody. He continued deferentially to peruse the glowing narratives of the missionaries, with their accounts of the superior Confucian morality and government, even if such panegyrics did not awaken in him the excited echoes they roused on the Continent. When Le Comte's *Memoirs and Observations* appeared in 1697, Confucius in the role of the good governor, the apostle of order and reason, was already a familiar figure.

This dependence of Judgements [said Confucius] by which the Stupid are subjects to the Learned, is very profitable and useful in

[31]Temple, *Works*, III, 456–57, "Of Ancient and Modern Learning." See also Homer H. Dubs, "A Comparison of Greek and Chinese Philosophy," *Chinese Social and Political Science Review*, XVII, No. 2 (July, 1933), 307–27.

[32]Temple, *Works*, III, 476.

Humane Society: Were all Families equally Rich, and equally
Powerful, there would remain no form of Government. But there
would happen yet a more strange Disorder, if Men were equally
knowing, every one would be for governing, and nobody would
believe himself obliged to obey.[33]

Human nature, would he often say, came from Heaven to us most
pure and perfect; in process of time, Ignorance, the Passions and
evil Examples have corrupted it; all consists in the reinstating it,
and giving it its primitive Beauty: and that we may be perfect, we
must re-ascend to that point from whence we have descended.
Obey Heaven, and follow all the Orders of him who governs it.
Love your Neighbor as yourself; never suffer your Senses to be
the Rule of your Conduct, but hearken to Reason in all things: It
will instruct you to think well, to speak discreetly, and to perform
all your actions holily.[34]

All but the most atrophied Tories or the most extreme
Whigs could have taken such political dicta within their stride.
The doctrine of reason and natural morality was a far more
slippery topic. Unquestionably it appealed to Temple, but he
judged Confucianism primarily by its political manifestations.
It was a philosophy for statesmen and for bringing about a
near heaven on earth. Whether it could exalt men to a more
lasting paradise was a question he left discreetly unexplored.
Continental authors, however, faced the problem more boldly.
Le Vayer and Leibniz had found only praise for the natural
morality of Confucius. Le Comte, Jesuit though he was, could
not restrain his enthusiasm:

China for two thousand years had the knowledge of the true God,
and have practis'd the most pure Morality, while Europe and almost all the World wallow'd in Error and Corruption.[35]

Though the Jesuit's memoirs were condemned by the faculty
of theology in Paris, such heresies could not be readily stamped

[33]Le Comte, *Memoirs and Observations*, p. 196.
[34]*Ibid.*, p. 199.   [35]*Ibid.*, p. 317.

out. Skepticism of revelation and formal religion was already rampant. Early studies in comparative religion had already begun, and such works as André Michel Ramsay's *Les Voyages de Cyrus* (1727), widely reprinted in England, showed a widening admiration for the heathen sages.[36] Rationalists revered a universe of inexorable mathematical order which allowed no place for the miracles, priestcraft, and superstition that clouded most religions. It was necessary to scrape them off like barnacles to discover the residuum of reason and real religion underneath. In this process of dissecting pagan sects Ramsay found their dogmas essentially those of Christianity, and in his "Discourse upon the Theology and Mythology of the Pagans" annexed to *Les Voyages* he paid particular tribute to the Chinese as he did in his later work, *The Philosophical Principles of Natural and Revealed Religion*.[37]

The basic premise of Ramsay's *Les Voyages* is essentially that of Tindal's *Christianity as Old as Creation* (1731), the Bible of deism, as Leslie Stephen called it.[38] This second great English champion of Confucius and the Chinese was similarly concerned to prove that religions of nature, whether in China or Peru, are basically the same. Writing in the popular didactic form of a dialogue, Tindal asserted that God at all times had given men sufficient means of knowing whatever He required of them, the "observation of those duties to God and men which reason dictates."[39]

To sum up all in a few words; as nature teaches men to unite for their mutual defense and happiness, and government was insti-

[36]See Albert Cherel, *André-Michel Ramsay, un aventurier religieux au XVIIIe siècle*, Paris, 1926.

[37]Andrew Michael Ramsay, *The Philosophical Principles of Natural and Revealed Religion*, Glasgow, 1748–49.

[38]Sir Leslie Stephen, *A History of English Thought in the Eighteenth Century* (New York, 1927), I, 134–63.

[39]Matthew Tindal, *Christianity as Old as Creation* . . . (Newburgh, 1798), heading of Ch. II.

tuted solely for this end; so to make this more effectual, was religion, which reaches the thoughts, wholly ordained; it being impossible for God, in governing the world, to propose to himself any other end than the good of the governed; and consequently, whoever does his best for the good of his fellow creatures, does all that God or man requires.[40]

The materialism of such a doctrine dovetailed neatly with Confucian morality, and Tindal's scathing disapproval of superstition and priestcraft in all its manifestations would have won him the sympathy of the literati. Doubtless he sensed this likeness among men of reason, for in describing the universal code of practical morality he found the sayings of Confucius and Christ almost interchangeable.

I am so far from thinking the maxims of Confucius and Jesus Christ to differ, that I think the plain and simple maxims of the former, will help to illustrate the more obscure ones of the latter, accommodated to the then way of speaking.[41]

Pursuing this argument, Tindal quoted with approval Leibniz' suggestion that the Chinese send missionaries to Europe to teach natural theology. The literati were, after all, as David Hume was to remark in his essay *Of Superstition and Enthusiasm,* "the only regular body of Deists in the universe."[42] It was nonetheless perhaps for the best, Tindal ultimately concluded, that this august body had not honored Europe with a visit.

Navarette, a Chinese missionary, agrees with Leibniz and says that "It is the special providence of God that the Chinese did not know

[40]*Ibid.,* pp. 24–25.   [41]*Ibid.,* p. 296.
[42]David Hume, "Of Superstition and Enthusiasm," in *Essays Moral, Political, and Literary,* ed. T. H. Green and T. H. Grose (London, 1898), I, 149.

what was done in Christendom; for if they did, there would be never a man among them, but would spit in our faces."[43]

A Europe split by political and religious schisms could not but be displeasing to a visitor from that empire of moral and political harmony over which brooded the giant figure of Confucius.

As depicted in one of the engravings of Du Halde's *Description . . . de la Chine* (1735),[44] a compilation of twenty-seven missionary accounts, Confucius is a grave, bearded Augustan, almost imperceptibly slant-eyed, meditating majestically in a neatly shelved European library of calf-bound books. Around this figure the Chinese legend had slowly accumulated. Dr. Johnson, in the course of his puffing for Cave's English edition of Du Halde, wrote with enthusiasm of Confucius.[45] The sage had become generally admired as the representative of an efficiently run patriarchy and the spokesman for a sensible morality almost Euclidean in its logic and efficiency.

For a long time he remained almost unshaken on his pedestal. The eighteenth century reissue of the *Morals* included a greatly enlarged account of his life. Alexander Pope in *The Temple of Fame* nodded politely in his direction.[46] His extensive biography in *The Chinese Traveller* (1775)

[43]Tindal, *Christianity as Old as Creation*, p. 348.

[44]There were two English versions of Jean Baptiste Du Halde's *Description . . . de la Chine*, 4 vols., Paris, 1735. One translation was published by John Watts in four volumes in 1736; the other, in two folio volumes by Edward Cave in 1738–41. These translations are discussed in Tsen-Chung Fan, *Dr. Johnson and Chinese Culture*, London, The China Society, 1945.

[45]Dr. Johnson is conjectured to be the author of an article which appeared in *The Gentleman's Magazine*, Vol. XII, in June-July-September, 1742. The section published in July deals in part with Confucius. See also Tsen-Chung Fan, *Dr. Johnson and Chinese Culture*, pp. 10 ff.

[46]Alexander Pope, *The Temple of Fame*, ll. 107–8. In *The Guardian* 173 Pope discusses Temple's essay "Of Gardening" which is also referred to in his letter to Robert Digby of August 12, 1723.

and Sir William Chambers' House of Confucius at Kew attested to his persistent fame. But even Confucius was vulnerable to attack, and the China which his morality dominated and which his followers governed was regarded with increasing skepticism and mistrust.

CONFUCIUS
Du Halde, 1735

THE IDOL VITEK

Montanus, 1671

IV

THE DISSENTING
OPINION

*I*N 1704 the papal bull of *ex illa die* declared against the
Jesuit interpretation of Confucianism,[1] but even before this
China had become suspect. Little by little the slow but persistent erosion of China's reputation, and, indirectly, that of
Confucius, had already begun. A highly articulate faction
challenged the enthusiasm of Temple, Tindal, and the Jesuits,
and, in spite of the prevailing admiration for Confucius and
his sect, they remained stubbornly unconverted. The wonders
of China, dazzling as they might be, could not paralyze
their critical instincts.

While the enthusiasm for the sage did not fever Europe till
the 1680s when the Jesuit translations began to appear,[2] even
before that the rigidly orthodox had begun to feel uneasy.
As early as 1667 Richard Baxter had detected a dangerous
drift from the thorny ways of virtue to the primrose paths
of heterodoxy. A reluctant admirer of the Confucian literati,
he found them, nevertheless, deniers of the immortality of the
soul.[3] Both he and Berkeley shared a low opinion of other
Chinese religions, which struck the latter as highly regret-

[1]Kenneth S. Latourette, *A History of Christian Missions in China* (New
York, 1929), pp. 146–47. Arnold H. Rowbotham, *Missionary and Mandarin* (Berkeley, 1942), pp. 165 ff.

[2]Louis Pfister, *Notices biographiques et bibliographiques sur les Jésuites
de l'ancienne mission de Chine: 1552–1773*, Shanghai, 1932–34. Arnold
H. Rowbotham, "The Impact of Confucianism on Seventeenth Century
Europe," *Far Eastern Quarterly*, IV, No. 3 (May 1945), 224–42.

[3]Richard Baxter, *The Reasons of the Christian Religion* (London, 1667),
p. 200.

table, mere sorceries and raptures, "Pythagorean fopperies."[4]

A mingled admiration and mistrust also marked the feelings of the last of the Stuart kings. While on a surprise trip to Oxford, James II visited the Bodleian and fell into conversation with its learned curator, Dr. Hyde, the Orientalist.

Then his majesty told Dr. Hyde of a book of Confucius translated from China language by the Jesuits (4 in number) and asked whether it was in the library? To which Dr. Hyde answer'd that it was, and that "it treated of philosophy, but not so as that of European philosophy." Whereupon his majesty asked whether "the Chinees had any divinity?" To which Dr. Hyde answered, "Yes, but 'twas idolatry, they being all heathens, but yet that they have in their idol-temples statues representing the Trinity, and other pictures, which shew that antient Christianity had been amongst them." To which he assented by a nod. After that, his majestie left off asking any more questions.[5]

His Majesty had evidently heard enough.

If the doctrine of Confucius was suspect, the more elusive ones of Buddhism and Taoism were still more so. His Majesty's subject, Captain William Dampier, during his 1687–88 stopover in the Orient, felt no intellectual curiosity about Confucianism and noted with distaste the habitual sacrifices made by Chinese merchants and seamen to their idols. His experience with an ignorant Chinese peasant who tried to persuade him to pay homage at a ruined forest shrine confirmed his opinion that their religious beliefs were ludicrous idolatry.[6] The Jesuits themselves made no effort to condone these practices. On his voyage through the Indian Ocean Louis Le Comte felt a growing horror as he watched the mariners

[4]*Ibid.* See also George Berkeley, *Works*, ed. Alexander C. Fraser (Oxford, 1901), II, 288. (Dialogue VI in *Alciphron*).

[5]*Life and Times of Anthony Wood* (Oxford, 1894), III, 236–37.

[6]*Dampier's Voyages*, ed. John Masefield (London, 1906), I, 394.

make their obeisance to black, smoking idols.[7] Buddhism and Taoism as represented in seventeenth century engravings and narratives were clearly designed to astonish and appall. When Defoe detailed in fascinated horror the homage of a mandarin and his retinue to a headless idol, equipped with claws and wings, he was mocking beliefs that most of the enemies of China found, on the whole, too palpably grotesque to attack.[8] The danger, these critics felt, lay not so much in these discredited sects as in the insidious and all-too-reasonable cult of Confucius.

Such men as William Wotton consequently struck directly at the sage himself. A comparison of the morality of the ancients and moderns convinced him that the teachings of Mango Capac, Mahomet, and Confucius fell pitifully short of those of Christ. The morality of China's sage he found no more than a pastiche of maxims "which good Sense and tolerable Experience might have furnished any Man with."[9] The French scholar, Eusebius Renaudot, took virtually the same stand. In his *Dissertation on Chinese Learning* (Paris, 1718; London, 1733) he dismissed the ritualistic books as "the science of a gentleman usher,"[10] and described the discrepancy between Confucius and Christ as so vast that it was futile to attempt to compare their maxims.

What we are taught by Jesus Christ is too well grounded to want the concurrence of Chinese Philosophy; and if any believe it may perfect the Mind and reform the Manners, though they know nothing thereof but by paraphrases, as obscure as the Text; they

[7]Louis Le Comte, *Memoirs and Observations* . . . , 3d ed. (London, 1699), pp. 7–8.

[8]Daniel Defoe, *Serious Reflections during the Life and Surprising Adventures of Robinson Crusoe* (London, 1895), pp. 119–20.

[9]William Wotton, *Reflections upon Ancient and Modern Learning* (London, 1694), p. 145.

[10]Eusebius Renaudot, *Dissertation on the Chinese Learning* (London, 1733), p. 234.

are advised to inquire into what may be objected to the Antiquity of this proud Nation, to their History and their Philosophy.[11]

It was a conclusion with which Daniel Defoe piously concurred. He infinitely preferred the religious beliefs of Mexico and Peru to the sage's macaronics of "polity, morality and superstition huddled together."[12]

Although the battle precipitated by Tindal's *Christianity as Old as Creation* centered around the basic premises of deism, Chinese religious thought was the subject of some minor skirmishes. In pushing the speculations of Tindal to their logical conclusions, Conyers Middleton made, among others, the ironic proposal that, since the religion of revelation was altogether superfluous, Christians might well turn instead to the doctrines of Mahomet or Confucius.[13] George Berkeley displayed a similar suave hostility. The "trifling and credulous" nature of the greater part of the Chinese hardly warranted his notice, but in *Alciphron* (1732) he took time to deplore the liberal interpretation afforded the writings of Zoroaster and Confucius and the searching scrutiny demanded in Biblical exegesis.[14]

Bolingbroke's first enthusiasm for Chinese religious doctrine declined as his conviction increased that the halcyon days had passed and that the inheritors of the wisdom of Confucius had succumbed to the wiles of Li Lao Kium (Lao-Tse) and Fo (Buddha).

The true principles of religion being removed, and these fantastic principles placed in lieu of them, the foundation of all religion is sapped at once. They who cannot persuade themselves that the religion they see practised is a service fit to be paid to a Supreme Being, nor consequently required by any such being, slide easily

[11] *Ibid.*, p. xxxvii.

[12] *Serious Reflections*, p. 117.

[13] Conyers Middleton, *A Letter to Dr. Waterland* (London, 1752), p. 168.

[14] Berkeley, *Works*, II, 261 (Dialogue VI in *Alciphron*).

from the belief that there is no religion, to the belief that there is no God. This happened in China, where the literati, or learned men, are, in truth, a sect of atheists, and theism seems to be the portion of the vulgar alone.[15]

This blunt disapproval is echoed in Dean Lockier's dismissal of the Chinese philosophers as all "Atheists, a sort of Spinosists,"[16] a term Bolingbroke, Bayle, and Malebranche likewise used to describe them.

The indictment culminates in the anonymous *An Irregular Dissertation Occasioned by the Reading of Du Halde* (1740) in which the author not only censures the atheism of the literati and the superstition of the vulgar, but dismisses Confucius with the remark: "In plain Truth the Rules of Morality are not intricate. Confucius, Plato, Epictetus and Plutarch only give you back the Dictates of your own Heart."[17]

The assault on China was broadened to include also an attack on its government. The most notable critic in this respect is Daniel Defoe who, throughout his career, in all his references to this country, displayed a persistent antagonism that varied from deceptive irony to downright invective.[18] In the *Further Adventures of Robinson Crusoe* (1719), he praised the justice of a hearing before a Chinese judge, but found little else to commend in their much-vaunted government.[19] *Serious Reflections during the Life and Suprising Adventures of Robinson Crusoe* (1720) found him still less indulgent toward a tyranny which functioned only through

[15] Henry St. John Bolingbroke, *Works* (Philadelphia, 1841), IV, 266–67.

[16] Joseph Spence, *Anecdotes and Observations and Characters of Books and Men*, 2d ed., ed. Samuel Singer (London, 1858), p. 52.

[17] Anonymous, *An Irregular Dissertation Occasioned by the Reading of Father Du Halde's Description of China* (London, 1740), p. 30.

[18] Ch'en Shou-yi, "Daniel Defoe, China's Severest Critic," *Nankai Social and Economic Quarterly*, VIII, No. 3 (October, 1935), 511–50; Paul Dottin, *Daniel Defoe et ses romans* (Paris, 1924), pp. 340–42.

[19] Daniel Defoe, *Further Adventures of Robinson Crusoe* (Oxford, 1927), III, 150 ff.

hasty judgments, lightning-like punishments, and remorseless executions.[20]

How he arrived at these views is debatable. Perhaps his distaste was a reaction to the panegyrics of Le Comte. His main informant, Captain Dampier,[21] felt comparatively indifferent toward China and its officials. He had touched it only tangentially[22] and had suffered none of the indignities that so nettled Captain Weddell and, later on, Captain Anson. Defoe's impatience with this government seems, consequently, a strong personal reaction rather than a literary inheritance. As a true-born Englishman and a zealous promoter of trade, he resented a government which was self-sufficient, exclusive in policy, and looked upon bustling Whig merchants as undesirable barbarians.

The author of *An Irregular Dissertation* shared, in part at least, Defoe's antipathy. It is difficult, however, to say to what extent, for his *Dissertation* in addition satirizes Walpole and the English government.[23] But he also regarded the Chinese government as an inflexible tyranny based on one maxim— the will of the prince.[24] Of the efficiency of the courts he felt small assurance. He doubted whether the head of the Exchequer could match in shrewdness the Jew in Change-Alley, or the Board of Rites rival the College of Heralds. Such comments are clearly as double-edged, as is his proposal to overcome Chinese ignorance in the subtle manipulations of statesmanship by sending a brace of English ambassadors and ambassadresses to Peking for breeding purposes.[25]

[20]Defoe, *Serious Reflections*, pp. 120–21.

[21]Willard H. Bonner, *Captain William Dampier* (Stanford, 1934), pp. 90–92.

[22]*Dampier's Voyages*, I, 402–8.

[23]Tsen-Chung Fan, "Chinese Fables and Anti-Walpole Journalism," *Review of English Studies*, XXV (April 1949), pp. 141–51.

[24]Anonymous, *An Irregular Dissertation*, p. 23.

[25]*Ibid.*, pp. 28–29.

More often than not, however, the Chinese government continued to be praised and used as a convenient means of satirizing the corruptions of the English government.[26] But in still a third respect China was continuingly attacked. Since the mid-seventeenth century the champions of orthodoxy had tried to integrate Mosaic and pagan history. If the Chaldean and Egyptian accounts were troublesome, those of the Chinese were still more so. The futility of the attempt to integrate these histories, pagan and Christian, led to a distrust of the Chinese annals and an attempt to discredit Chinese pretensions to mastery of mathematics and astronomy. On these the validity of the annals depended.

The Jesuits, though by 1700 they had trumpeted loud and long the wisdom and antiquity of the land they hoped to convert, nevertheless failed to persuade William Wotton, for one, to credit the authority of Martin Martinius and the missionaries in matters of chronology. The English scholar was anything but impressed by China's knowledge in mathematics, mechanics, and medicine.[27] The papal bull of *ex illa die*, invalidating the Jesuit interpretation of Confucian rites, heightened disbelief of the missionaries' eulogies, and it is not altogether coincidental, perhaps, that the most blistering criticism of China's antiquity and learning appeared the year after the papal edict.

Defoe's early work, *The Consolidator* (1705), despite its deceptive opening praise of China, was nevertheless bitterly hostile. Its paean to a land of an ancient, wise, polite, and ingenious people quickly slipped into ludicrous overpraise and ridicule.[28] The author sneeringly cited the three hundred and sixty-five volumes of Augro-machi-lanquaro-zi and the pre-

---

[26]Fan, "Chinese Fables," *Review of English Studies*, XXV, 141–51. This material is also discussed in Chapters V and VII, below.

[27]Wotton, *Reflections upon Ancient and Modern Learning*, pp. 144–54.

[28]Defoe, *Works* (Oxford, 1840), IX, 210 ff.

tended histories of two thousand emperors. He taunted the Laputa-like scientists who hoped to convert hogs' eyes into glasses so penetrating that one could see the wind with them. He cited the two hundred and sixteenth volume on navigation written two thousand years before the deluge by the learned Miracho-lasmo who claimed a lunar origin. (He was perhaps a relative of Domingo Gonzalez, Bishop Francis Godwin's Man in the Moon, who, after a voyage to a lunar Utopia, had been deposited in China by his swan-drawn machine.)[29] Such wisdom, Defoe suggested, was not to be wondered at. In addition to their inheritance of extraplanetary wisdom, the Chinese had been blessed with a far-seeing emperor, Tangro XV, who had mercifully preserved their cultural heritage by providing them with a fleet of 100,000 ships to escape the deluge.

Now if it be true, as it is hinted before, that the Chinese empire was peopled long before the flood, and that they were not destroyed in the general deluge in the days of Noah; it is no such strange thing that they should outdo us in this sort of eyesight we call general knowledge, since the perfections bestowed on nature, when in her youth and prime, met with no general suffocation by that calamity.[30]

Not apparently satisfied with this ridicule of a race of intellectual charlatans, Defoe could not resist damning them briefly in Serious Reflections.[31] As mechanics he estimated them far below those of Europe. Even as artisans the Chinese displeased him, for he stripped them of their last pretensions by attributing their preeminence in porcelain and lacquer work not to superior craftsmanship but to superior raw materials.

Sweeping as Defoe's condemnation of its antiquity and

[29]Francis Godwin, The Man in the Moone (London, 1638), p. 114.
[30]Defoe, Works, IX, 244.
[31]Serious Reflections, pp. 120 ff.

learning may have been, it was without documentation. But mathematicians and astronomers were not lacking to seek tangible proof of the falsity of China's pretensions. It was for these men to test Bernard Mandeville's suspicions that the Chinese histories were "fifty times more extravagant and incredible than anything contained in the Pentateuch."[32] In doing so they began to sift the Chinese astronomical computations, the chronology included in *Confucius Sinarum Philosophus,* and Foucquet's table of Chinese history.

Typical of the attempts to prove these annals fabulous, and the ancient kings of Cathay chimerical, is a letter from George Costard to the Royal Society.[33] From beginning to end he ridicules Chinese astronomy—the belief that an eclipse occured when a dragon swallowed the sun, the gap of 1379 years in the annals during which no eclipses whatsoever were recorded, and the accounts of an imaginary conjunction of seven heavenly bodies. He also points out, as many others did, a striking paradox. How was it, if the Chinese were such masterful and accurate astronomers, that it had proved necessary to call in the Jesuits to compute the calendar and help staff the observatories?

An occasional scientist might seek to make an accord between Oriental and Occidental calculations by pointing out that the Chinese word "year" denoted the revolution of a planet around the heavens, and that their figures required readjustment,[34] but derogatory analyses of the Chinese annals were far more frequent, and the histories which had so delighted seventeenth century polymaths were treated by their descendants with disbelief and contempt.

[32]Bernard Mandeville, *The Fable of the Bees* (London, 1806), p. 489.
[33]*Philosophical Transactions of the Royal Society,* XLIV (April-May 1747), pp. 476–92. Chinese chronology and astronomy are also considered in the transactions of September-October 1730, pp. 397–424, and in the transactions for June 1753, pp. 309–17.
[34]*The Gentleman's Magazine,* XIV (January, 1744), 55.

By 1750 China was no longer generally esteemed among English intellectuals either for its antiquity or learning. At the beginning of his career Dr. Johnson had exclaimed that the Chinese were a people "perfectly polite, and completely skilled in all sciences."[35] The morality of Confucius at first also appealed to him. But as the years passed,[36] his opinions altered; his projected Chinese stories never appeared, and his attitude became progressively more antagonistic. When during one of Boswell's inquisitions he counseled the peppery Scot to read *Bell's Travels* and visit The Great Wall, he was prompted largely by perversity. On a later occasion he felt less indulgent. A reference to the East Indians as "barbarians" furnished Boswell with a fine opening.

BOSWELL. "You will except the Chinese, Sir?" JOHNSON. "No, Sir." BOSWELL. "Have they not arts?" JOHNSON. "They have pottery." BOSWELL. "What do you say to the written characters of their language?" JOHNSON. "Sir, they have not an alphabet. They have not been able to form what all other nations have formed." BOSWELL. "There is more learning in their language than in any other, for the immense number of their characters." JOHNSON. "It is only more difficult for its rudeness, as there is more labor in hewing down a tree with a stone than with an axe."[37]

With Temple the Chinese vogue among men of letters had reached its height. With Johnson it was in the decline. The literary cult of China and the flowering of *chinoiserie* in the minor arts did not coincide in England as they did in France.[38]

[35]The quotation is from the preface to Dr. Johnson's translation of Father Lobo's *Voyage to Abyssinia* (1735). For Johnson's interest in China see Tsen-Chung Fan, *Dr. Johnson and Chinese Culture*, London, The China Society, 1945.

[36]See note 45 in Chapter III.

[37]James Boswell, *Life of Johnson*, ed. George B. Hill (New York, 1887), III, 386.

[38]Adolf Reichwein, *China and Europe*, New York, 1925; Henri Cordier, *La Chine en France au XVIIIe siècle*, Paris, 1910; Pierre Martino,

When the apostrophes of Voltaire and Quesnay reached their height,[39] the Chinese vogue among English intellectuals was already dying. True, throughout the eighteenth century it continued to attract some notice.[40] Swift gave it passing attention,[41] and Addison in *The Spectator* made graceful occasional use of the subject.[42] (One of Steele's happiest *jeu d'esprits*, a supposed letter from the Emperor to the Pope, asking for one of his nieces as a concubine, has even been accepted as genuine by some later writers.)[43] But China had no strong intellectual partisans among English men of letters after the days of Temple and Tindal. By 1750 its preeminence in the sciences had been generally discredited, and praise of its antiquity had declined though many still applauded its government, and the morality of Confucius was politely admired. When China was mentioned it was chiefly as a source of pleasant amenities. Thus Dr. Johnson, in his maturer years, despite his vanished admiration for the Far East, waxed

---

L'Orient dans la littérature française au XVIIe et XVIIIe siècle, Paris, 1906.

[39]Lewis A. Maverick, "Chinese Influences upon the Physiocrats," *Economic History*, III, Nos. 13–15 (February, 1938), 54–67; "The Chinese and the Physiocrats: a Supplement," *ibid.*, IV, No. 15 (February, 1940), 312–18; "Chinese Influences upon Quesnay and Turgot," *Claremont Oriental Studies*, No. 4, June, 1942; and *China: a Model for Europe*, San Antonio, 1946.

[40]Shau Yi Chan, "The Influence of China on English Culture during the Eighteenth Century," *Chicago University Abstract of Theses*, 1927–29, Humanistic Series, pp. 537–41; Tsen-Chung Fan, "Chinese Culture in England from Sir William Temple to Oliver Goldsmith," *Harvard University Summaries of Ph.D. Theses*, 1931, pp. 223–26; Ch'ien Chung-shu, "China in the English Literature of the Eighteenth Century" (in two parts), *Quarterly Bulletin of Chinese Bibliography*, II, Nos. 1–2 (1941), 7–48; II, Nos. 3–4 (1941), 113–52.

[41]Jonathan Swift, *Prose Works*, ed. Temple Scott, London, 1897–1908. See the following: I, 79, 87; VIII, 58, 140; XI, 10.

[42]*The Freeholder*, No. 4; *The Guardian*, No. 96; *The Spectator*, Nos. 189, 414, 415, 511, 584, 585.

[43]*The Spectator*, No. 545. L. Carrington Goodrich in his review of Eloise Hibbert's *Jesuit Adventures* (see *Far Eastern Quarterly*, I, No. 2, February, 1942, 185–86) clearly shows this letter to be an imposture.

lyrical in his defense of tea.[44] It was at least one product of China to which he had hopelessly succumbed. Others felt the allure of delicate porcelains and gilded and lacquered furniture. The occasional visitors from the Middle Kingdom were socially lionized. Not least of all, exotic stage spectacles kept the English interest in China alive.

[44]Samuel Johnson, *Works,* ed. Arthur Murphy (London, 1816), II, 333–48.

V

SCENES AND

FESTIVALS

Cʜɪɴᴀ's ʟᴏɴɢ ʙᴜᴛ ꜰɪᴛꜰᴜʟ ʀᴏʟᴇ in the English theatre dates from January 1, 1604. James I, newly ascended to the throne, proposed to dazzle the French ambassador with a magnificent entertainment, and to that end his masquers had assembled in the great hall where the torches and candelabra outblazed the stars.

On New Yeares night we had a play of Robin goodfellowe and a maske brought in by a magicien of China. There was a heaven built at the lower end of the hall, owt of which our magicien came downe and after he had made a long sleepy speech to the king of the nature of the cuntry from whence he came comparing it with owrs for strength and plenty, he sayde he had broughte in cloudes certain Indian and China Knights to see the magnificency of this court.[1]

The wearisome prologue served as a foil to set off the impressive spectacle that followed. One by one the masquers entered, all of the highest rank, and advancing toward the sovereign they presented him with a sonnet, and a jewel worth forty thousand pounds. James accepted the gem languidly. He was secretly negotiating for its purchase, but he feigned on this occasion to receive it as a gift from his subjects. How much this apparent opulence impressed the French ambassador we do not know, but the chronicler of the event maliciously

---

[1] E. K. Chambers, *The Elizabethan Stage* (Oxford, 1923), III, 279. See also I, 171.

records that the French King "would have been well pleased with such a present, but not at this prise."[2] The presentation accomplished, the Indian and Chinese masquers resumed their dances, although their costumes were so cumbrously rich with laced satins, and their hats so loaded with feathers and jewels, that they had difficulty executing the changes. But with a wave of the magician's wand the enchantment was dispelled. The masquers resumed their identities, and the masque dissolved, as it had begun, to music. The Indian and China masquers had accomplished their purpose. They were ambassadors from the Cathay of Polo and Mandeville, and having presented their gift, they vanished like apparitions.

Almost as ephemeral are the references to China in Elizabethan and Caroline drama. At the beginning of the seventeenth century the Ottoman empire was still the most powerful in the world, and when the Elizabethans looked Eastward their eyes were focused on the Turks and the Moors.[3] Both of these types they depicted with some accuracy, but other Eastern races merged into a vague composite, and, though Elizabethan playwrights made passing mention of China's porcelains, its cities and Great Wall, its learning and religion, nowhere did they specifically make use of Chinese characters or settings.[4] China, to the average playgoer, was *terra incognita*. It had little value either in the bustling Jacobean comedy of realism or the psychological Italianate tragedy of intrigue.

With the rise of the heroic drama, however, playwrights deliberately sought out distant settings and remote historical episodes. Heroic emotions, they found, flourished in the

[2]*Ibid.*, III, 279.

[3]Louis Wann, "The Oriental in Elizabethan Drama," *Modern Philology*, XII, No. 7 (January, 1915), 423–47.

[4]Robert Cawley, *The Voyagers and Elizabethan Drama* (Boston, 1938), pp. 208–31.

rarefied atmosphere of Peru, India, or the Orient.[5] Exalted sentiments that would have seemed conspicuously out of place at the court of Charles II seemed somehow almost credible in the courts of Montezuma or before the Dragon Throne.

When Elkanah Settle completed *The Conquest of China* (1676),[6] a dramatization of the fall of the Ming dynasty, he claimed history and truth as the basis of his drama.[7] He did not hesitate, however, to tailor and embroider the web of fact. Martin Martinius, Juan de Mendoza, and Peter Heylyn had amply documented the Tartar conquest,[8] but Settle was less concerned with writing an historical drama than in adapting these materials to the pattern of the heroic play. The results were not altogether happy. Though three years in gestation, the finished work, as Shadwell suggested, hardly indicated it.[9] Even the rehearsals foreshadowed failure. Ludicrous incidents took place in the course of enacting such stage directions as "They all fall on their swords,"[10] and the dismal failure of the play in Dorset Garden can have surprised no one.[11]

In the opening scene Zungteus, heir to the Tartar rule, is confronted with the classic dilemma of heroic drama. The Tartars are at war with the Chinese, but Zungteus is in love with a Chinese girl, curiously named Amavanga. How is he

[5]T. Blake Clark, *Oriental England* (Shanghai, 1939), pp. 61 ff., discusses China's subsequent role in eighteenth century English drama.

[6]Frank C. Brown, *Elkanah Settle* (Chicago, 1910), p. 17, claims this play was acted before February, 1673/4. Alfred Harbage, *Annals of the English Drama* (Philadelphia, 1940), p. 136, suggests its production was in 1675.

[7]Epilogue to *The Conquest of China*, London, 1676.

[8]Martin Martinius, *Bellum Tartaricum*, London, 1655; Juan Gonzalez de Mendoza, *The History of the Great and Mighty Kingdom of China*, ed. Sir George Staunton, London, 1853–54; Peter Heylyn, *Cosmography*, 5th ed., London, 1677.

[9]Preface to *The Libertine*, London, 1676.

[10]John Downes, *Roscius Anglicanus*, ed. Montague Summers (London, 1928), p. 35.

[11]John Genest, *Some Account of the English Stage* (Bath, 1832), I, 170.

to obey the dictates of love yet fulfill his father's orders to lay waste his beloved's native land? His problem is unexpectedly resolved when, in a clash between the two armies, he unwittingly kills Amavanga who has disguised herself as a soldier. Overcome with remorse, he meditates enlisting on the side of his enemies, who are harassed not only by the Tartar invasion but by civil war as well. In the course of a blood bath of epic proportions ("The scene opens, and is discovered a Number of Murdered Women, some with Daggers in their Breasts, some thrust through with Swords, some strangled, and others Poyson'd; with several other Forms of Death"),[12] Lycurgus, a treacherous mandarin, seizes the Dragon Throne, but his forces are compelled to flee before the conquering armies of Zungteus. The Tartar prince restores order, Amavanga reappears, miraculously healed of her wounds, and the triumphant couple ascend the throne of China together.

The action is as violent, the heroic couplets as relentless, and the characters' behavior as unnaturally motivated as any in the worst of the heroic dramas. In addition, history is ruthlessly distorted. Certainly it offers no parallel for Settle's Boadicea-like heroine, though Nieuhoff in his account of the conquest mentions a lady of "heroic virtue," and her name, Amavanga, may be derived from "Amavang" in Bouvet's account of K'ang Hsi.[13] The name of the Tartar prince, Zungteus, is a Latinization of Zung-teh, and in the rebellious Lycurgus we can trace perhaps the bandit Li Tzu-ch'eng who so plagued the last of the Ming emperors. But Settle's version of this epic catastrophe is as inadequate to the theme as must have been the eighteenth century French shadow-play, *La Conquête de la Chine.*[14]

[12]*The Conquest of China,* V, ii.

[13]Joachim Bouvet, *The Present Condition of the Muscovite Empire* . . . *with the Life of the Present Emperor of China* (London, 1699), p. 22.

[14]Henri Cordier, *La Chine en France au XVIIIe siècle* (Paris, 1910), p. 91.

The failure of this play did not, however, deter another author from attempting the same topic. Sir Robert Howard completed his play on this subject soon after, if we may conjecture from a letter written by John Dryden, his brother-in-law, to his sons at Rome in September of 1697.

After my return to town, I intend to alter a play of Sir Robert Howard's, written long since, and lately put by him into my hands: 'tis called "The Conquest of China by the Tartars." It will cost me six weeks study, with the probable benefit of an hundred pounds.[15]

Dryden abandoned the project soon after, and how much, if any, of the revision he completed is conjectural. The whereabouts of the original manuscript is unknown, and only a fragmentary scene of "Sir Robert Howard's play" exists. On the strength of the 1697 letter Nicoll attributes this scene to Dryden;[16] inasmuch as it is bound in a volume with the manuscript of the Earl of Rochester's *Valentinian,* and both are in the same hand, John Haywood, Rochester's editor, assigns it to the Earl.[17] As it stands, the fragment is an isolated episode, impossible to place in relation to the main action of Howard's play.

In it we are faced, as in Settle's play, with an Amazonian heroine shouting heroic couplets to exhort her Chinese armies to victory. Hyachian and Lycurgus, her two commanders, are also rivals for her love. Since she favors the former, Lycurgus prepares to betray his country's cause, and the scene concludes as Hyachian feverishly urges the army on and salutes the empress for her valor.

In this short fragment the author shows some real poetic

[15]John Dryden, *Works,* ed. Scott and Saintsbury (London, 1893), XVIII, 133–34.

[16]Allardyce Nicoll, *Times Literary Supplement,* Jan. 13, 1921, p. 27.

[17]John Wilmot, *Collected Works,* ed. John Haywood (London, 1926), pp. xv-xvi.

power and some skill in characterizing the proud, ambitious Lycurgus (whose name is reminiscent of Settle's villain), the valiant and youthful Hyachian, and the tempestuous empress, who is more interested in fighting than in receiving elaborately wrought compliments. Although the characters bear superficial affinities to those in the earlier play on the same theme, the pace and texture of the verse could not be more different. That of the isolated scene is controlled and rapid; that of the Settle play hysterical and disjointed. Lost heroic plays go, for the most part, deservedly unwept, but this fragment makes us regret that the projected alteration of the Howard play was never completed.

Despite the failure of these serious plays on a Chinese theme, Settle apparently felt a continuing interest in the subject. In that pastiche, *The Fairy Queen* (1692), with music by Purcell and a libretto based on *A Midsummer Night's Dream*, he made use of China once more,[18] this time purely for purposes of pageantry and display. As in the early masque presented before James, the langorous songs and dances of the Chinese contrasted effectively with the witty antics of Robin Goodfellow. Hack-writer though he was, Settle had a keen sense of the theatre and was among the first to appreciate the East as a rich source of dramatic coloring. His skillful use of the resources of the theatre resulted in an entertainment that enjoyed a success with both the court and the town. But so prohibitive was the cost of the scenic novelties and ornaments, superior, Downes tells us, even to those of *King Arthur* and *The Prophet*, that despite its popularity it made little profit for the company.[19]

The spectacular nature of *The Fairy Queen* is evident from

[18]For a discussion of Settle's authorship see Allardyce Nicoll, *Times Literary Supplement*, March 15, 1923, p. 180; Brown, *Elkanah Settle*, p. 96.

[19]Downes, *Roscius Anglicanus*, pp. 42–43, 247.

the songs and dances and the climactic Chinese diversion inserted into Shakespeare's patched and mangled text. So established did many of its features become in later entertainments of this sort, that its stage directions merit some attention. Designed to exhaust all the possibilities of the Restoration theatre, those of the fifth act reached a spectacular climax:

While the Scene is darken'd, a single Entry is danced; Then a Symphony is play'd; after that the Scene is suddainly illuminated, and discovers a transparent Prospect of a Chinese Garden, the Architecture, the Trees, the Plants, the Fruit, the Birds, the Beasts, quite different from what we have in this part of the World. It is terminated by an Arch, through which is seen other Arches with close Arbors, and a row of Trees to the end of the view. Over it is a hanging garden, which rises by several ascents to the top of the House; it is bounded on either side with pleasant Bowers, various Trees, and numbers of strange Birds flying in the Air, on the top of a Platform is a Fountain, throwing up Water, which falls into a large basin.[20]

The details are pleasantly vague, reminiscent of the vaporous landscapes of *chinoiserie,* and obviously calculated to give any imaginative scenic designer *carte blanche.* In such a setting Purcell's lovelorn Chinese serenade each other in conventional lyrics made piquant by the introduction of foreign names:

Yes, Xanxi, in your Looks I find,
The charms by which my heart's betrayed.[21]

To soothe their distraction six monkeys come from between the trees and dance, followed by a hymeneal chorus and a climactic scenic marvel: "Six pedestals of China-work rise from under the Stage; they support six large vases of Porcelain, in which are six China Orange-Trees."[22] Songs and dances

[20]*The Fairy Queen.* V, ii.   [21]*Ibid.*   [22]*Ibid.*

by the reconciled lovers, Chinese and Shakespearean, bring the entertainment to a close.[23]

The stage career of *The Fairy Queen* was not, however, at an end.[24] Purcell's exquisite score, perhaps the most beautiful of his four operas, led to a successful London revival in 1945, apparently the first complete public performance since the original production. Many of the spectacular aspects of its concluding scene were, however, copied again and again. The pedestals of China work and porcelain vases reappeared in *The Chinese Festival* (1755). The dance of the monkeys became such a feature of these entertainments that a later satirical essayist proposed a Chinese ballet of "the best dancers now in Asia, whether monkeys or men."[25] When Mozart's score for a court entertainment in the Chinese style was recently discovered and revived as a ballet by Michel Fokine, the conventional "danse des singes" was introduced.[26] The stream of porcelain princesses that have fluttered across the stage in ballets and extravaganzas needs no comment.

The success of Settle's *The Fairy Queen* was due, of course, only in part to this Chinese tincture, but the fifth act made a particular appeal to contemporary audiences. William and Mary had brought with them from Holland a strong taste for things Chinese, and in the last decade of the century the essays of Temple and the narratives of the Jesuits had brought the Chinese into prominence. The rage for Orientalia was not long in developing and was soon satirized in the theatre. In Charles Burnaby's *The Ladies Visiting Day* (1701), ostensibly directed at Francophiles, the author also satirized the more *recherché* tastes of Dolt and Lady Lovetoy, apostles of alien

[23]For a discussion of this production see George C. Odell, *Shakespeare from Betterton to Irving* (New York, 1920), I, 71–72, 150, 192–95.
[24]A one-act musical version was given at Drury Lane on Feb. 1, 1703.
[25]*The World*, No. 205, Dec. 2, 1756.
[26]*L'Epreuve d'amour*, René Blum Ballets, 1936.

fashions and lovers. Despising her British gallant, Lady Lovetoy justified her abusive treatment of him thus:

Ha! he deserves no other—But in India and China those Softnesses never touch the Men; They remain in their native Strength and Simplicity, tho' all things about 'em be so fine and delicate; their Silks, their Networks, little Baskets, Calicoes—they contrive the greatest Trifle so prettily, and can make a habit as the French do a dish of Meat, or a Discourse, out of nothing![27]

In contrast, Burnaby drew the picture of Fulvia, a girl of homespun English tastes, who, with the young hero, succeeds in bringing the apes of fashion to their senses.

In 1705, in his only comedy, *The Biter*, Nicholas Rowe expounded a similar theme. Sir Timothy Tallapoy has returned from the East irretrievably converted to its luxuries and manners. As Nabob of Kingquancungxi, he has amassed a fortune, and his infatuation with the Orient is such that he is dressed and served in the Chinese fashion. The plot involves his efforts to marry off his daughter to an undesirable "biter." The situation is a standard one, but what lends the play its novelty is the picture it gives of the "foreignized" Englishman. Betterton himself chose to play this part, which is amusingly conceived from the start. In it Rowe makes fun of the Chinese pretensions of all kinds. Sir Timothy boasts of his pagode of Callasusu, "who was nephew to the great Fillimaso, who was descended from the illustrious Fokiensi, who was the first inventor of eating rice upon platters."[28] He rails at the corruption of the times:

I will comfort myself after the manner of the sage Philosopher Tychung, who liv'd Fifteen Thousand Seven Hundred and Fourteen Years Two Months and Three Days Ago, and let the world rub. . . . I will send forthwith to my correspondent at Canton for

[27]*The Ladies Visiting Day*, II, i. [28]*The Biter*, II, i.

a new Pagode. . . . I will marry my daughter to the young man I have provided for her . . . and after that I will incontinently espouse the most amiable Mariana, and engender a Male Off-Spring, who shall drink nothing but the Divine Liquor Tea, and eat nothing but Oriental Rise, and be brought up after the institutions of the most excellent Confucius.[29]

As the victim of folly, he receives the traditional comic reward: the appropriate couples are united, despite his objections, and he departs angrily for the East Indies.

Rowe's play is an amusing one, and if it failed[30] it was because he had anticipated his audience. Produced forty or fifty years later, it would have enjoyed an almost certain success. The vogue had not yet reached its full tide. Occasional playwrights, however, continued to find Oriental backgrounds useful. In his Preface to *The Fatal Vision* (1716), Aaron Hill observed:

Our distance from, and dark ideas of, the Chinese nation, and her borders, tempted me to fix my scene in so remote a location. The fable is fictitious; and the characters are all imaginary.

Such a locale had its conveniences. It offered opportunities for imaginative dresses and scenes. In such a remote clime heroes and heroines could storm, rant, and suffer, undisturbed by the exigencies of more realistic settings.

As in Settle's play, violence and surprise punctuate Hill's story of Uncham, Emperor of China and usurper of the throne of Siam, and Ipanthe, daughter of the deposed king, who, with her lover, Orontes, plots to recover the throne and free the state. At the climax of the action, as the young lovers accomplish their purpose, Selim, a favorite eunuch of Uncham's, is revealed as the Emperor's wife, long believed dead,

[29]*Ibid.*
[30]David Erskine Baker, *Biographia Dramatica* (London, 1782), II, 32.

and Orontes, the conspirator, is unmasked as their long-lost son and the prophesied conqueror of his father.

Hill's play was acted at Lincoln's Inn Fields with success, due largely, no doubt, to the new costumes and decor.[31] His plot, despite his deference to Gildon and the unities, is as tangled and improbable as that of the next Chinese-English play, Michael Clancy's *Hermon, Prince of Choraea* (1746). In this dramatization of a multiple assault on the Chinese throne, history and chronology are wildly disordered. Fohi (Fu Hsi), the legendary Chinese Emperor, is reincarnated as a young Tartar prince, the leader of one faction. Koxinga, the seventeenth century marauder who troubled the Manchus, is rechristened in this play as Icaon, the commander of still another faction. In the midst of this chaos walks the hero, Hermon, a slant-eyed Hamlet, meditating revenge for a sister, soliloquizing on his inadequacy, and gloomily pondering his claim to the throne.

Needless to say, the play was unacted. As a friend of the author observed in the published prologue:

> His play seems built on a fantastique Topick,
> And for the Scene, that's—somewhat near the Tropick;
> His nymphs are China-Ware; East-India Queens;
> His Heroes, painted Pagods—fit for Screens.

The judgment was all too accurate. The author could not invest his creatures with any semblance of realism. They merely stepped off the screens and China-ware to play their parts in this hodgepodge of revenge and rebellion. In telescoping history the author made his plot almost inextricably complicated, though his play, like Settle's, has at least the merit of unflagging, if confusing, action.

But the tragic woes of these attenuated heroic dramas

---

[31] Genest, *Some Account*, II, 583.

bored the middle-class audiences of the eighteenth century, and the exotic elements were transferred increasingly to the spectacles and pantomimes which culminated in Garrick's disastrous *Chinese Festival* of 1755. Why the Orient played such a part in these spectacles is evident to anyone who has seen the seventeenth century folios on the Far East. Kircher's *La Chine* and Nieuhoff's *Embassy* abound in plates depicting processions, ceremonies, and gorgeous equipages. Such festivals as the Feast of Lanterns attracted much attention in England and on the Continent. Characteristically, Reichwein finds, the French court ushered in the eighteenth century with Chinese festivities.[32] Oriental costume became common in the *fêtes galantes* they loved so well. Bonnart, Martin, and Boquet have left many drawings for these, and in Rameau's *Les Indes galantes* Indian and Chinese knights mingled as indiscriminately as they had in the earlier Jacobean masque.[33] As early as 1723, at the Foire St. Germain, a pantomime was being performed—*Arlequin Barbet, pagode et mandarin*, the tale of a Chinese princess wooed by a Japanese prince, and his valet, Harlequin.[34] This piece by Lesage and D'Orneval had its successor in 1729 in the Foire St. Laurent's *Le Chinois de retour* and *Le Chinois poli en France* (1734). In addition to these amusements, Chinese shadow-plays were introduced into France by way of Germany, the Théâtre de Seraphim Dominique presenting a large repertory of them.[35]

In England as well, China played a part in the popular pantomimes.[36] Of these diversions, the most transient of all entertainments, we know little, but doubtless they also featured

[32]Adolf Reichwein, *China and Europe* (New York, 1925), p. 22.

[33]Many of these designs are reproduced in Cyril W. Beaumont's *Ballet Design Past and Present*, London, 1946.

[34]Cordier, *La Chine en France*, pp. 125–27.

[35]*Ibid.*, p. 91.

[36]Samuel McKechnie, *Popular Entertainments through the Ages*, London, 1931, discusses the rise of pantomime.

the pomp and trappings of the East. Devoid of dialogue, they amalgamated music, dancing, and mime. The first of these is, significantly, of French origin—*Arlequin Docteur Chinois* (1720),[37] followed four years later by *Harlequin Invisible; or, The Emperor of China's Court*.[38] William Chetwood's *The Emperor of China Grand Volgi; or, The Constant Couple and Virtue Rewarded*, labeled a dramatic opera but not printed, was performed at Bartholomew Fair in 1731,[39] probably to compete with the spectacular scenic effects of the conjurer Hawkes, who was performing there at the same time. This entertainment may have made some pretense to authentic atmosphere, for Chetwood, in addition to being a Grub Street dramatist, was also a bookseller and the author of three vast fictional narratives, based largely on Dampier and contemporary collections of travels.[40]

Whatever idea of China such entertainments conveyed was doubtless of little importance. The audience wanted music, laughter, and transformation scenes, and as long as Harlequin's baton conjured up the Emperor of China's palace where formerly a peasant's hut had stood, they remained satisfied.

During the 1750s when the Chinese madness reached its height, the production of such pantomimes also reached its climax. John Rich, whose skill in transformation scenes Pope had acknowledged in *The Dunciad*,[41] offered such serious opposition to David Garrick that the latter was compelled to hire Henry Woodward to rival him.[42] Under Woodward's direction *Proteus; or, Harlequin in China* was produced at

[37]Allardyce Nicoll, *A History of Early Eighteenth Century Drama, 1700–1750* (Cambridge, 1929), p. 402.

[38]*Ibid.*, p. 373. [39]*Ibid.*, p. 306.

[40]Willard H. Bonner, *Captain William Dampier* (London, 1934), pp. 183–92.

[41]*The Dunciad*, III, 257–60.

[42]Elizabeth Stein, *David Garrick, Dramatist* (New York, 1938), p. 110.

Drury Lane on January 4, 1755.[43] Perhaps the then prevailing vogue brought forth other pantomimes now not even known by title, for John Shebbeare the contemporary satirist commented: "The Chinese taste is so prevalent in this city at present, that even pantomime has obliged Harlequin to seek shelter in an entertainment where the scenes and characters are all in the taste of that nation."[44] Likewise, Colman and Thornton in *The Connoisseur* noted Harlequin's travels to China[45] and commented wearily on the frequency of Chinese dress in masquerades.[46]

Such was the appeal of these entertainments that it seriously disturbed David Garrick. The "monstrous pantomimes" seemed perilously close to silencing Shakespeare, Otway, and Rowe.[47] Woodward's entertainments had not achieved a sufficient success, and Garrick found himself forced to make concessions to a public that longed for the exhibitions of Rich. To satisfy these demands, he went to unusual lengths. Rumors had reached him of the immense success enjoyed in France by Jean George Noverre's ballet *Les Fêtes chinoises*, and, in the latter part of 1754, he had begun negotiation for a London production.[48] According to contemporary description, the appeal of this spectacle was similar to that of *The Fairy Queen*. With sets by Boucher and costumes by Boquet, it introduced eight rows of mandarins and slaves dancing together, followed by a procession of Chinese musicians and palanquins drawn by white and black slaves. While these joined in a round dance, the scene shifted from the exterior of

[43]Genest, *Some Account*, IV, 406.

[44]John Shebbeare, *Letters on the English Nation*, 2d ed. (London, 1756), II, 263.

[45]*The Connoisseur*, No. 76, July 10, 1755.

[46]*The Connoisseur*, No. 66, May 1, 1755.

[47]Arthur Murphy, *The Life of David Garrick* (Dublin, 1801), p. 180.

[48]Thomas Davies, *Memoirs of the Life of David Garrick* (London, 1780), I, 177.

a palace to the interior of a porcelain shop where, as in
The Fairy Queen, porcelain vases miraculously arose to con-
ceal the dancers.[49]

The success of the ballet had, however, turned the choreog-
rapher's head, and Noverre, from the beginning, proved himself rapacious in his dealings with Garrick. In addition to
asking three hundred and fifty guineas for himself, he insisted on bringing his wife, the designer Boquet, and the
dancer De Laître.[50] By the time he had arrived in August,
1755, he had assembled a company of approximately a hundred.

Plans for the production were seriously ill-timed. England
and France hovered on the brink of war. Wits and scribblers
were quick to make capital out of this foreign "invasion," and
the essayists at that moment were concentrating their fire
on the Chinese madness. The arrival of the foreign dancers
provoked a storm of criticism. The whisper spread that the
leading dancer was actually the disguised Dauphin and the
remainder of the cast were in reality French officers.[51] To
counteract these ominous rumblings, Garrick advertised in
the London newspapers, explaining that Noverre was a Swiss
Protestant and his wife a German, and hopefully and extrava-
gantly he continued his plans to eclipse the success of the
Paris version.

The production had its first night on November 8, 1755, at
Drury Lane.[52] Oppressed by a premonition of disaster, Garrick invited the King to attend, in the hope that his august
presence might insure an untroubled performance. The sovereign, who had never seen Garrick act, consented, and the

[49]Frank A. Hedgcock, *David Garrick and His French Friends* (London,
1912), p. 128 (footnote).

[50]*Ibid.*, pp. 129–30.

[51]*Journal Étranger* (Paris, December, 1755), pp. 223–35.

[52]Genest, *Some Account*, IV, 442–44.

evening began without incident.[53] The monarch was received with good humor by the audience, but after the preliminary performance of *The Fair Quaker of Deal,* and the beginning of *The Chinese Festival,* the whistles and catcalls began. The nobility frowned, but the tumult continued, and the King, informed that it was merely because the people hated the French, smiled enigmatically and withdrew as the gallery gods raised the shout, "No French dancers!"

The four subsequent performances were marred with incidents of a more serious nature.[54] The nobility took up the dancers' cause and drew swords against the rioters. A man fell from the gallery into the pit. One objector was hurled down three flights of stairs. At one performance not a note of music could be heard, as the nobility had repaired on that evening to the Opera, and the dancers were left without partisans in an audience which demolished chandeliers, threw chairs, and swarmed menacingly into the pit toward the stage. The wings filled with armed actors and stagehands, the tank below the stage was flooded, and the rioting continued until the audience received a promise that *The Chinese Festival* would not be performed again. The following evening the returning nobility demanded a repetition of the ballet despite the violent opposition of the rest of the audience, and Garrick, brushing aside the pleas of his partner Lacy, who had been persistently against continuing it, agreed to produce it the next evening.

On Tuesday, November 18, Drury Lane was packed three hours before performance time, with an audience singing patriotic songs and hoarding rotten apples. No sooner had the performance begun than tumult broke out. The dancers

[53]For an account of these riots see Hedgcock, *David Garrick,* pp. 131–35; Davies, *Memoirs,* I, 179–83; Murphy, *Life of Garrick,* pp. 179–83; Percy Fitzgerald, *The Life of David Garrick* (London, 1868), I, 310–20.

[54]Genest, *Some Account,* IV, 443–44; Hedgcock, *David Garrick,* pp. 131–35.

fled among a storm of missiles. The dissenting aristocracy discreetly withdrew, and the rioters, satisfied with their success at the theatre, swarmed through the streets and indulged in the final satisfaction of breaking every window in Garrick's house.

When the offending manager appeared on the stage three days later, he threatened to quit the stage unless permitted to perform unhindered. His courage won back the audience's affection, but his project had dismally failed, with a loss of some four thousand pounds.[55] According to one critic this had all been wasted, for a duller entertainment had never been seen,[56] though such a verdict is doubtful in view of Garrick's good theatrical taste and the fine dancers he employed. At least one happy result of the debacle was the profound influence which Garrick exercised upon Noverre, which led the latter to develop the ballet pantomime (*ballet d'action*) in place of ballet which depended on stately movement.[57]

The demise of the spectacle in which they were mutually involved was the result of many factors. Unquestionably the first of these was the current hostility toward the French and the roaring patriotism which decried anything foreign. Rival managers may have been responsible for packing the audience with hostile spectators.[58] The ballet also came at a time when the satirists were attacking grotesque *chinoiserie* with venomed quills. The combination of these factors was overwhelming. So great was Garrick's failure that with the single exception, perhaps, of *The Mandarin; or, Harlequin Widower* (1789), Chinese entertainments of this sort were driven from the stage for the remainder of the century.[59]

Only one serious play on a Chinese theme was produced

[55]Genest, *Some Account*, IV, 444.
[56]Davies, *Life of Garrick*, I, 183.
[57]Hedgcock, *David Garrick*, p. 144.
[58]Fitzgerald, *Life of Garrick*, I, 313, 317.
[59]Allardyce Nicoll, *A History of Late Eighteenth Century Drama*, 1750–1800 (Cambridge, 1927), p. 335.

during this period. This was Arthur Murphy's *The Orphan of China* (1759), an English adaptation of a genuine fourteenth century Chinese play of the Yuan dynasty.[60] Murphy's version had, however, a complicated genesis, and forms one of a group of contemporary adaptations. Its Chinese original, *The Orphan of the House of Chao*, was first translated by Father Premaré into French and included in Du Halde. Though Premaré deleted whole passages from the original, he kept the thread of the dramatic narrative unbroken, and his version attracted enough interest to be reprinted separately in 1755. It appeared also in English, German, and Dutch translation, and in English, French, German, and Italian adaptations.

The first of the English adaptations, inspired by Du Halde, was that of William Hatchett, who found in this tale of an orphan's revenge against a power-mad minister of state a suitable vehicle for an attack on Walpole. But whether his adaptation, *The Chinese Orphan*,[61] was ever acted is doubtful. Primarily it was intended as a political pamphlet, as the dedication to the Duke of Argyll, Walpole's political enemy, makes quite clear.

In Hatchett's version, China, the land of ideal government, is plagued by Siako, an infamous mandarin, who in addition to his crimes against the state succeeds in almost totally exterminating the family of his political rival. One by one they perish, with the exception of a newborn child who escapes when Kifang, a patriotic physician, substitutes his own child for the doomed infant. The orphan is accepted as Kifang's own son. The prime minister, unaware of the substitution, and in gratitude to Kifang for his services, intercedes with the emperor to adopt Kifang's son. Ironically he works his

[60]Ch'en Shou-yi, "The Chinese Orphan: a Yuan Play," *T'ien Hsia*, III, No. 2 (September, 1936), 89–115.

[61]William Hatchett, *The Chinese Orphan*, London, 1741.

own destruction. A painted robe is prepared for the presentation of the child, detailing the whole of Siako's infamy, the king's eyes are opened, and the disclosure brings torture and death to the evil minister.

Whereas in Du Halde's version the child reaches maturity and wreaks his own revenge, in Hatchett's version the role of the orphan and the theme of personal revenge are minimized. Siako becomes the focal figure in the play; his downfall, though effected by a ruse, is depicted as a matter of public necessity. But despite this change of stress in the plot, Hatchett took much material directly from Cave's English edition of Du Halde. Some scenes—Act I, scenes 3, 4, and 5, and Act II, scene 1—are almost *verbatim* transcriptions. Similarly he adopted the device of interspersing songs "after the Chinese manner." One suspects that the political possibilities of this plot revealed themselves to the author in the course of his adaptation. The first three acts adhere fairly closely to the source. Only in the last two acts is political criticism introduced, and the last act, in particular, is weakened considerably by retelling the whole plot to emphasize Siako's perfidy. Hatchett's treatment of this character is not wholly unsympathetic, however. Siako is made to feel some doubts, some quiverings of conscience, and his soliloquies on the misuse of power evoke faint recollections of the troubled musings of Claudius and Macbeth.

Hatchett's knowledge of China itself appears to have been no greater than that of Settle or Hill. Ousanguey (General Wu San-kuei in charge of the Chinese forces at the time of the Tartar conquest) appears in this play as a friend of the benevolent physician. The orphan is renamed Cam-Hy (K'ang Hsi), and the sage old courtier becomes Lao-Tse, though a gap of some two thousand years separated the emperor and the philosopher. In addition, Hatchett slips into amusing anachronistic references to the royal purple.

If Hatchett erred in these minor matters, his right to trans-
form the material as he saw fit would have been upheld by
many. In his Preface he praised the play for strokes of nature
scarcely equaled in the European drama, but he shared the
general opinion that the play contained some blemishes. This
was still, after all, the period of "Shakespeare improved."
Surely it was admissible to embellish lesser plays?

The Orphan of the House of Chao had, however, a strong
enthusiast in Bishop Hurd who detected in the play laudable
resemblances to Greek drama.[62] In it he found the essentials of
dramatic poetry, and action which was unified and began
as close to the catastrophe as possible. The natural dialogue
pleased him. His enthusiasm led him to draw parallels between it and Sophocles' *Electra* in its motive of revenge, its
moral expressions, and, at heightened moments, songs, "somewhat resembling the ancient chorus." If common sense had
led the Chinese to this identity of composition with the drama
of the Greeks,

what effects must it not have in more enlightened countries and
times, where the discipline of long experience, and criticism
(which is improved common sense) come in to the assistance of
the poet? Under these advantages, the strictest conformity may
well be thought the result of common principles, which yet we
agree to explode under the opprobrious name of imitation.[63]

Later he qualified his praise still further. Perhaps he felt
he had spoken too warmly, for his critique of the Chinese
drama, which was published in the first edition of his *Com-
mentary on Horace's Epistle to Augustus*, was dropped from
subsequent editions.

Voltaire, in his 1755 version of the play, showed a similar

[62]Richard Hurd, *Discourse on Poetical Imitation*, London, 1751. The
section on the Chinese drama was extracted and reprinted in Thomas
Percy's *Miscellaneous Pieces Relating to the Chinese* (London, 1762),
I, 215–32.

[63]Percy, *Miscellaneous Pieces*, I, 231–32.

approach, at once admiring and patronizing. In both the Chinese and Greek theatre he saw the same spontaneous line of development.[64] He felt, however, that the Oriental play needed a final polishing from the eighteenth century man of enlightenment and taste. The time-pattern distressed him, and he found the over-all plot in need of reorganization to make it conform to the unities. Like Hatchett, he truncated the plot so that the orphan remained a child throughout the action. Like Hatchett also, he did not stress the theme of revenge. Instead, he lent his play a philosophic tone, and in his Preface styled it a dramatization of the morals of Confucius. Echoing his oft-expressed admiration for China, it was intended as answer to Rousseau's thesis that science and art corrupt natural morality.[65]

Without doubt it was this version by Voltaire and Hurd's *Discourse* that induced Arthur Murphy to write his own adaptation.[66] In all probability he had consulted also the version completed by Dr. Thomas Francklin for the English edition of Voltaire which he and Smollet had prepared.[67] Though in his prefatory letter Murphy acknowledged his prime debt to the sage of Ferney, he did not passively accept *in toto* Voltaire's version. The former introduced two new characters to further the action of the drama, and under his hands a treatise on morals and government became a melodrama. In Murphy's version the climactic action of the play also took quite a different turn. Timurkan, the Tartar emperor, usurper of the Dragon Throne, instead of falling under the spell of the wisdom and antiquity of an alien civilization, died an unrepentant tyrant's death.

[64]Voltaire, *Oeuvres Complètes* (Paris, 1877–85), V, 289–358.

[65]*Ibid.*; see Épitre Dedicatoire, V, 296.

[66]Murphy's debt to Voltaire is discussed in John P. Emery's *Arthur Murphy* (Philadelphia, 1946), pp. 49–50.

[67]See *Works of Voltaire*, tr. Smollett, Francklin, and others (London, 1763), Vol. XXVII.

Before its successful production, this version precipitated a long and stormy struggle between Garrick and Murphy.[68] The story of this theatrical feud is a long one, fraught with promises, altercations, and renewed promises. The play had been completed by 1756, but Garrick, doubtless still smarting from *The Chinese Festival*, seemed indisposed to present it. Ultimately, the favorable opinions of William Whitehead, Henry Fox, and Horace Walpole prevailed, and the play was produced in 1759. Furnished with magnificent sets, salvaged perhaps from the fiasco with Noverre, it marked the successful debut of Mrs. Yates, and enjoyed periodic revivals.[69] Though its characters lack humanity and rave in the stilted blank verse of the period, the play is well constructed. Murphy skillfully carpentered the Voltaire and Du Halde versions and restored the original dramatic interest of the play. The critics were generally favorable, and Goldsmith, in *The Critical Review*, somewhat reluctantly added his voice to the chorus.[70]

In view of the fact that Goldsmith was shortly to enjoy his first literary success with *The Citizen of the World*, his attitude was curiously anti-Chinese. He praised Voltaire for not adhering to the Chinese outlines of the fable, and for "deviating from the calm insipidity of his Eastern original."[71] Inasmuch as Murphy had deviated still further from the original, Goldsmith found his version so much the more perfect. Goldsmith was clearly not in sympathy with William Whitehead's sentiments expressed in the Prologue to Murphy's play:

> Enough of Greece and Rome. Th'exhausted store
> Of either nation now can charm no more. . . .

[68]For detailed accounts of this see Howard H. Dunbar, *The Dramatic Career of Arthur Murphy*, New York, 1946; *The Private Correspondence of David Garrick*, 2 vols., London, 1831–32.

[69]Genest, *Some Account*, IV, 549; V, 46–47; VI, 15–16.

[70]Oliver Goldsmith, *Works*, ed. Peter Cunningham (Boston, 1900), VII, 253–60.

[71]*Ibid.*, p. 254.

On eagle wings the poet of tonight
Soars for fresh virtues to the source of light,
To China's eastern realms: and boldly bears
Confucius' morals to Britannia's ears.[72]

The remaining English version of the Chinese play is that
of Thomas Percy who in his *Miscellaneous Pieces Relating to
the Chinese* (1762) made a literal translation from the French
version of Du Halde that retained the directness and charm
of the original. Still other adaptations of this story included
Metastasio's *L'Eroe Cinese* (an operatic treatment) and
Goethe's fragment *Elpinor*.

The multiplicity of these versions justified Du Halde's
selection of this play as most likely to appeal to Occidental
taste, despite his realization that it was not a Chinese play of
the highest order.[73] For nearly a century, however, it remained
the only one of its kind known in Europe. Though Percy included the rough outline of another Chinese play in his *Hau
Kiou Choaan* (1761),[74] and there are sketches of Chinese
dramas in the later accounts by members of Lord Macartney's
embassy, it was not until J. F. Davis's nineteenth century
translation of *Laou-Seng-Urh* (*An Heir in His Old Age,*
1817)[75] that England possessed another authentic Chinese
play.

During the last half of the eighteenth century the tide had
turned. China was no longer fashionable and had little effect
on the stage. Harlequin bobbed up infrequently in Oriental
dress, and the orphan of the House of Chao occasionally
sought his revenge, but beyond this China made no further
impression on the late eighteenth century theatre. How tran-

[72]Prologue to Murphy's *The Orphan of China*.

[73]John Brown, *History of the Rise and Progress of Poetry* (Newcastle,
1764), pp. 222–23, discusses Du Halde's choice.

[74]Thomas Percy, *Hau Kiou Choaan* (London, 1761), Vol. IV.

[75]John F. Davis, *Laou-Seng-Urh or, "An Heir in His Old Age,"*
London, 1817.

sient was its contribution to the English stage of the seventeenth and eighteenth centuries is proved by Andrew Cherry's comic opera, *The Travellers* (1806).[76] Oxberry in his edition of the play tells us this Occidental-Oriental melange was permitted to pass with applause because of its music and dresses. Its stage directions are strangely reminiscent of earlier spectacles.

A beautiful garden in the Chinese style—with many bridges,—intersecting Canals, etc.—The Sun rising slowly in the distance. —The curtain is drawn up slowly to a symphony resembling the warbling of birds.[77]

As the fantastic plot unfolds, however, the similarities fade. The inhabitants of these picturesque landscapes are no longer apparitions like those of Settle's opera. They are closer to flesh and blood.

Prince Zaphimri, the heir to the throne of China, is sent abroad by his father to visit Europe and in particular England, "to scan those laws which wondering nations silently admire."[78] He is accompanied by his Eurasian beloved, Celinda, who sets out in quest of her long-lost father. Eventually they identify him as a distinguished English admiral, and, hand in hand, the lovers contemplate their mutual happiness and the wonders of the British legal system. The curtain rings down on the prince's paean to the British constitution.

The *rêve chinois* was over. Although the spectacular background of this comic opera is approximately the same as that in earlier Chinese entertainments, the author's attitude is entirely different. The prince's progress through Asia and Europe serves as an occasion for a series of varied scenes culminating in the triumph of Albion. China is transformed

[76]Oxberry's *New English Drama* (London, 1830), Vol. XVII.
[77]*The Travellers*, I, i.   [78]*Ibid.*, I, ii.

from an exotic land of wonder to a provincial empire eager to clasp the British constitution to its breast.

This last entertainment was not, of course, seriously intended, but with the exception of plays derived from *The Orphan of the House of Chao,* no serious attempts were made to understand China or the nature of its drama. Even the accounts of the travelers themselves showed an increasing hostility toward genuine Chinese entertainments. The entertainments and plays which had so diverted Ysbrant Ides[79] in 1692, struck members of Macartney's entourage, a century later, as "wretched dramas."[80] From 1760 on, China had little importance on the English stage. The heroic drama was defunct. Genuine Chinese plays were inaccessible, and the demise of *The Chinese Festival* had discouraged similar spectacles. Most significant of all, the fever of *chinoiserie* had by that time begun to run its course.

[79]John Harris, *Voyages and Travels* (London, 1744–48), II, 939.
[80]John Barrow, *Travels in China* (Philadelphia, 1805), pp. 139 ff. See also Sir George Staunton, *An Authentic Account of an Embassy . . .* (London, 1797), II, 30–31.

VI

ENGLISH

CHINOISERIE

*B*Y THE MID-EIGHTEENTH CENTURY the Chinese rage had infected England so completely that James Cawthorne, the satirist, lapsed into reproachful and almost plangent terms to describe the abjectness of the surrender:

> Of late, 'tis true, quite sick of Rome and Greece,
> We fetch our models from the wise Chinese,
> European artists are too cool and chaste,
> For Mand'rin only is the man of taste.[1]

Evidence of perverted standards confronted Cawthorne everywhere. Mandarins nodded on gilt chimney pieces, ladies fought over rare porcelains, cows reposed in Oriental barns, and Confucius presided over the calf-bound classics in the study.

The vogue that reached its fever peak in the 1750s had germinated in Tudor times when swarthy Portuguese sailors first brought the delicate Ming porcelains back to Europe. The Virgin Queene, mistress of a rival empire, rejoiced in such luxuries; nearly two centuries later her delight was echoed by Mrs. Montagu on the receipt of a gift of china, "six fine plates used by Elizabeth at breakfast."[2] The founding of the East India Company in 1600 promoted the taste for these novelties on a more extensive scale (as Pompey indicated in *Measure for Measure* by apologizing for his mistress' crock-

---

[1] James Cawthorne, "Essay on Taste" (1756), *Poems*, London, 1771.

[2] Reginald Blunt, *Mrs. Montagu: Queen of the Blues* (Boston and New York, 1924), I, 63.

ery: "They are not China dishes, but very good dishes"),[3] and by 1609 the first porcelain shop in London opened its doors.[4]

The growth of the taste for Oriental textiles took place at a somewhat later date, for the imports were expensive and more difficult to obtain than porcelain. But references to them occur in early Restoration diaries and letters. Evelyn succumbed to the passion for fine Oriental fabrics,[5] and Pepys shopped for chintzes to enliven his wife's study.[6] During the later days of the Stuarts so popular did these importations prove that native weavers forced legislation to prohibit their import. Nevertheless, the demand for the foreign products continued, and the smuggling of fabrics developed on so vast a scale that British weavers were provoked to riot.[7]

The early imports were not, however, limited to these two commodities. The restrictions on textiles did not prevent the trading ships from bringing back brilliantly lacquered cabinets and screens to decorate the apartments of such wealthy purchasers as Charles the Second's unpopular mistress, the Duchess of Portsmouth.[8] The appeal of such furniture appears to have been almost immediate, for as early as 1688 John Stalker's *Treatise of Japanning and Varnishing* was published, the first of a series of manuals on the fine art of lacquering later brought to perfection in France by the Martin brothers. Temporarily the term "japanning" took hold, in part because of the nonchalant confusion between the countries of the

[3]*Measure for Measure*, II, i, 97.

[4]B. Sprague Allen, *Tides in English Taste* (Cambridge, Mass., 1937), I, 193.

[5]John Evelyn, *Mundus Muliebris* (London, 1690), pp. 2–3.

[6]Samuel Pepys, *Diary*, ed. Richard, Lord Braybrooke (New York, 1884), III, 312, Sept. 5, 1662.

[7]Allen, *Tides in English Taste*, I, 218–33.

[8]John Evelyn, *Diary and Correspondence*, ed. William Bray (London, 1871), pp. 407–8; Oct. 4, 1683.

East,[9] and in part because much of the lacquered furniture was introduced to Europe by the Dutch East India Company, founded in 1602, whose trade was largely with Japan. Consequently, gaily decorated desks and commodes became generally associated with Japan rather than China, though they were imported from both countries.

In a review of the steady growth of *chinoiserie* in England the part played by these Dutch merchants must not be underestimated. Under the Stuarts the seeds of the vogue had been sown; under William and Mary it came into flower. They brought with them from Holland a decided taste for the luxuries of the East. Daniel Marot, the monarchs' architect, has left us drawings for a Chinese room, and through the Dutch-China idiom England received two of her leading decorative motifs—the eagle with outstretched wings, and the claw and ball foot of the imperial dragon.[10]

By the time of Anne, and later George I, the Chinese taste was widespread among connoisseurs. Earlier men of taste such as Evelyn had rejoiced in collections of Eastern curios,[11] and a love of the Orient had so dominated the mad Duchess of Albermarle that she had consented to marry the Duke of Montagu only after being persuaded that he was the Emperor of China.[12] Chief among the more rational enthusiasts was Elihu Yale, Nabob of Madras, and an intense and lifelong collector of *objets d'art*. At his death in 1721, Yale left his English heirs the accumulation of years in the East. His vast collections of paintings, cloths, muslins, silks, jewels, Indian and Japan cabinets, and Oriental works of art virtually crowded his harassed heirs out of the house. To disengage themselves they

[9]*Ibid*, p. 395; July 30, 1682.

[10]Oliver Brackett, *Thomas Chippendale* (London, 1924), p. 56.

[11]Evelyn, *Diary and Correspondence*, p. 264; June 22, 1664.

[12]Horace Walpole, *Letters*, ed. Mrs. Paget Toynbee (Oxford, 1905), XIII, 254; to Sir Horace Mann, March 8, 1775. This episode was later dramatized in Crowne's *Sir Courtly Nice*.

held forty auction sales, and England was exposed to Oriental goods on a scale hitherto unknown.[13]

The rage was further stimulated by a corresponding vogue in France, to which the founding of Colbert's 1660 Merchant Company and the Siamese embassy had given impetus.[14] That Le Roi Soleil, despite his classic taste and geometric preferences, felt the Chinese allure is evidenced by Le Vau's Trianon de Porcelaine at Versailles. If China did not approximate the Palladian ideals, it boasted at least a solidified culture, a properly hierarchical society, and an autocratic government which appealed to the French king. To Louis XIV's successors such considerations were perhaps secondary to the fact that this exotic art offered a relief from the mathematical rigidity of classicism. The soft, clinging silks and the delicately graded coloration of the Chinese porcelains complemented perfectly the rococo of the age of Louis XV.

In England, *chinoiserie* had the appeal of novelty and surprise.[15] Until the mid-eighteenth century it did not seriously threaten the classical ideals, and England was content to enjoy the amenities of the East. Tea, "the excellent and by all physitians approved China drink," was introduced in 1658, though at the prohibitive price of four guineas a pound.[16] The ebullient Pepys sampled it as a costly novelty,[17] but by 1743, Walpole tells us, tea had become a universal habit.[18] The popular-

[13]Hiram Bingham, *Elihu Yale* (New York, 1939), p. 313.

[14]Jacques Guerin, *La Chinoiserie en Europe au XVIIIe siècle*, Paris, 1911; Adolf Reichwein, *China and Europe*, New York, 1925; Henri Cordier, *La Chine en France au XVIIIe siècle*, Paris, 1910.

[15]There are many articles on this topic. See M. G. May, "Chinoiserie," *English*, II, No. 8 (1938), 96–105; Tsui Chi, "Chinese Influence on English Art," *Asiatic Review*, n. s., XXXIX (April, 1943), 195–99; Francis Lenygon, "The 'Chinese Taste' in English Decoration," *Art Journal* (July, 1911), pp. 193–98. Also John Steegman, *The Rule of Taste* (London, 1936), Ch. III.

[16]Agnes Repplier, *To Think of Tea!* (Boston, 1932), pp. 4–5.

[17]Pepys, *Diary*, I, 247; Sept. 25, 1660.

[18]Walpole, *Letters*, I, 319; to Sir Horace Mann, Jan. 13, 1743.

ity of China's porcelain, fabrics, wallpaper, and furniture was such that English and continental industries were quick to take advantage of the new market. The blue and white Delft earthenware of Holland had been available since 1625, but by the end of the century, a native English majolica had been developed at Bristol and Liverpool, and in 1745 the great Bow and Chelsea factories were in operation.[19] By 1746 Chinese-patterned wallpapers two yards long were available at London's Mincing Lane,[20] and lacquering and cabinetmaking had become an established branch of craftsmanship.

In the course of its Europeanization *chinoiserie* began to develop bizarre aspects. Decadent qualities soon manifested themselves as merchants traded on the eccentric tastes of porcelain collectors who eagerly sought out freak types. Unpainted porcelain was imported from Japan to be painted in Sino-European style with landscapes of willows, palms, and pagodas.[21] The fanciful Oriental world of the Dutch seventeenth century travel book engravings came to life in the textile patterns and porcelain ornamentations. Against highly stylized backgrounds, whimsical and capricious figures moved about in a strangely dimensionless world. An art at once so vaporous and frivolous allowed free play to the subtle fantasies of Watteau and Meissonier, but in the hands of lesser genius the treatment of such material led, more often than not, to grotesque extravagances.

In England this deliberate cult of the bizarre, this romantic protest against a frigid classicism, arose as the result of many

[19]There are many accounts of the development of English porcelain: William B. Honey, *English Pottery and Porcelain*, London, 1933; Marc L. Solon, *A Brief History of Old English Porcelain*, London, 1903; *The China Trade and Its Influences*, Metropolitan Museum of Art, New York, 1941; also Reichwein and Sprague Allen.

[20]Lenygon, "The 'Chinese Taste,'" *Art Journal* (1911), pp. 193–98.

[21]Allen, *Tides in English Taste*, I, 192–200.

factors.[22] The revolt had begun early in the eighteenth century with the canonization of Lorrain, Rosa, and Poussin, and the deposition of Le Nôtre as the arbiter of landscape gardening. The formal Dutch-French garden, with its knots and quincunxes, had given way to the more natural asymmetrical garden of Addison and Pope. The Gothic revival of the 1740s had struck still another blow at Augustan ideals.[23] It had released the imagination of the artist, in defiance of the reserved and impersonal ideals of classicism. Parallel to this Gothic anti-classic revolt was the cult of China, which was enjoying at the time general esteem as the home of superior morality and government and the source of agreeable luxuries. Chinese art had the virtue of being at once novel, remote, and intangible. Such advantages obviously appealed to the rebellious imaginations which had created serpentine garden walks in lieu of axial ones, and picturesque Gothic ruins in place of cool Corinthian columns. Behind correct Georgian façades the exponents of the new vogue created their own version of the bizarre and illusory world of China.

The progress of their pseudo-Chinese art was perhaps first evident in architecture. By 1740 Chinese pavilions had risen at Lord Lichfield's estate in Staffordshire and at Ranelagh.[24] A decade later William and John Halfpenny's *New Designs for Chinese Temples, Triumphal Arches, Garden Seats, Palings, etc.*, testified to the rapid evolution of this taste. Published in four parts, from 1750 to 1752, the later sections showed increasing elaboration in the designs for staircases, chairs, gazebos, and ceilings. Soon the drift of taste had become a flood tide. When Edwards and Darly published *A New*

[22]Arthur O. Lovejoy, "The Chinese Origin of a Romanticism," *Journal of English and Germanic Philology*, XXXII, No. 1 (January, 1933), 1–20.

[23]Arthur O. Lovejoy, "The First Gothic Revival and the Return to Nature," *Modern Language Notes*, XLVII, No. 7 (November, 1932), 419–46.

[24]Brackett, *Chippendale*, p. 57.

Book of Chinese Designs in 1754, they included plans of temples and hermitages, beds and girandoles—in addition to the engravings of Chinese landscapes, flowers, and figures—to serve as aids to decorators and designers.

The force of the movement was irresistible. In *The Architectural Remembrancer* (1751) Robert Morris, architect and champion of the Athenians, had vainly raised his voice against the storm. His *Select Architecture,* published at the height of the movement, reiterated his protest.

Gaiety, Magnificence, the rude Gothic, or the Chinese unmeaning Stile, are the study of our modern architects, while Grecian and Roman Purity and Simplicity are neglected.[25]

His cry went unregarded by the multitude that clamored after the new fashion, and Gothic and Chinese architecture continued to dominate the field. Eight years after the publication of the Halfpennys' work, books of this kind were still appearing: Charles Over's *Ornamental Architecture in the Gothic, Chinese and Modern Taste* (1758) and Paul Decker's *Chinese Architecture Civil and Ornamental* (1759).

The rage understandably spread from architecture to furniture design. Thomas Chippendale's *The Gentleman and Cabinet Maker's Director,* published in the same year as Edwards and Darly's designs, fathered a whole school of furniture. Though the plates of his book were engraved by Darly, Chippendale's biographers claim that his work had been completed earlier, and the great furniture maker developed his designs independently.[26] How practical these were meant to be it is difficult to say. Some undoubtedly were executed; many of them, like those of other furniture designers and architects, were never realized. Undoubtedly much of the *chinoiserie*

[25]Robert Morris, *Select Architecture* (London, 1755), Preface.
[26]Brackett, *Chippendale,* p. 58.

set down on paper failed to materialize either in the house or garden. Chippendale himself made some significant remarks on this score. In the Preface to his *Director* he vigorously de-

A CHINESE
RUSTIC CHAIR
Edwards and Darly
1754

fended himself against the charge that his designs of "household furniture in the Gothic, Chinese, and Modern Taste" could not be executed.[27] His successor, Robert Manwaring, likewise protested that the intricate and asymmetrical scrollery and embellishments of his own gilt mirrors, desks, and bookcases could be "easily executed by the Hands of a tolerably skilful Workman."[28] Both designers apologized with good reason. Many a gentleman and cabinetmaker must have suspected that the drawings were ingenious improvisations rather than practical designs.

Seduced though he was into the extremes of the movement, Chippendale's inventions had, nevertheless, a peculiar beauty. He created for the Duchess of Beaufort, a friend of Mrs.

[27]Thomas Chippendale, *The Gentleman and Cabinet Maker's Director* (London, 1754), Preface.

[28]Robert Manwaring, *The Cabinet and Chair-Maker's Real Friend and Companion* (London, 1765), Preface.

Montagu (whose house in Portland Square boasted a famous Chinese room), a rival salon at Badminton, with black lacquer and gilded furniture set against walls papered in pale pink.[29] He designed the famous Chinese bedroom in Claydon House, and the Chinese drawing room from Woodcote Park now in the Boston Museum of Fine Arts.[30] In such rooms he succeeded perfectly in capturing the wayward and fantastic character of *chinoiserie*. The Chinese style failed, however, basically to influence his designs. His green and gold furniture for David Garrick was, for example, Chinese only in ornamentation. But so strongly did these decorative embellishments stamp his productions between 1755 and 1760 that traces of them lingered in his work for many years. During the 1760s the Chinese blended with his Gothic designs, and in his later more classic period the capricious ornamentation still persisted, enlivening chairs of increasingly austere design.

The rage, while it lasted, had still other manifestations. To supplement exotic furnishings and architecture, enthusiasts called in foreign artists, steeped in the traditions of *chinoiserie*. Watteau, famous for his oriental arabesques, enjoyed success in England before achieving it in France.[31] Jean François Clermont, during his stay in England in the 1750s, adorned gardens with curious statuary, ceilings with airy *singeries*, and could number among his patrons Lord Radnor, Lord Northumberland, Walpole, the Duke of Marlborough, and the Prince of Wales.[32] Jean Pillement, painter and decorator, enjoyed an unqualified success in London with his flower pieces and landscapes. His fanciful engravings continued to

[29]Tsui Chi, "Chinese Influence on English Art," *Asiatic Review*, n. s., XXXIX (April, 1943), 198.

[30]Eben H. Gay, *The Chinese Room from Woodcote Park*, Boston Museum of Fine Arts, 1928.

[31]Louis Dussieux, *Les Artistes Français à l'Etranger* (Paris, 1856), p. 134.

[32]*Ibid.*, p. 139.

DOME BED IN THE CHINESE STYLE

Chippendale, 1754

From the Collection of Avery Library

be published after the Seven Years' War, despite the decline of the vogue and hostility to the French. Between 1758–1760 no less than six of these series of studies appeared.[33]

Strange wallpaper birds and flowers covered the dark paneled oak. Pagodas rose in place of antique temples. "Degenerate" silks and muslins replaced good solid homespuns. Curious specimens of china littered the shelves of lacquered and gilt cabinets. The desecration spread even further. It went beyond the bounds of the household. It attacked the outside world of nature.

The part which the Chinese garden played in the development of eighteenth century English landscaping has been copiously discussed in many books.[34] Unanimously their authors revert to Sir William Temple as the first exponent of the asymmetrical *sharawadgi*[35] garden style, "where the beauty shall be great, and strike the eye, but without any order or disposition of parts that shall be commonly or easily observed."[36] However, during the years following the publication of his essay, while the English natural garden slowly developed, similarities and dissimilarities between English and Chinese theories were forgotten. Temple's discusson of *sharawadgi* was paraphrased in the *Spectator* (No. 414), but the term was not revived until after 1752. It was at this time that the trans-

[33]Désiré Guilmard, *Les Maitres ornemanistes* (Paris, 1880), II, 188–89. See also Dussieux, *Les Artistes français*, p. 141.

[34]Elizabeth W. Manwaring, *Italian Landscape in Eighteenth Century England*, New York, 1925; Eleanor von Erdberg, *Chinese Influence on European Garden Structures*, Cambridge, Mass., 1936; Ch'en Shou-yi, "The Chinese Garden in Eighteenth Century England," *T'ien Hsia*, II, No. 4 (April, 1936), 321–39.

[35]This term is discussed by Y. Z. Chang, "Sharawadgi," *Modern Language Notes*, XLV, No. 4 (April, 1930), 211–14; E. V. Gatenby, *Times Literary Supplement*, Feb. 15, 1934, p. 108; Mary Quan, "Chinese Influence upon Eighteenth Century Gardening," unpublished Master's Essay, Columbia University, 1948, Ch. IV.

[36]Sir William Temple, "Of Gardening," *Works* (London, 1814), III, 237.

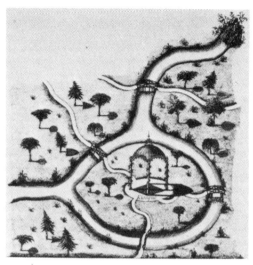

GARDEN DESIGN
Le Rouge, 1776–85
From the collection of Avery Library

DECORATIVE ENGRAVING
Montanus, 1671

Pl. 54. — The Elevation of a Temple partly in the Chinese Taste.

TEMPLE PARTLY IN THE CHINESE TASTE
Halfpenny, 1752
From the collection of Avery Library

lation of Father Attiret's description of the summer palaces of Yuan-ming-Yuan appeared. First published in the 27th Recueil of *Lettres édifiantes et curieuses* (1749), the Jesuit's account aroused enormous interest, and Joseph Spence's English translation was widely reprinted in the periodicals.[37]

Attiret's description of the Emperor of China's pavilions and pleasure gardens, their canals and serpentine paths, delighted English readers. The account of the court painter to K'ang Hsi[38] appeared to authenticate the fragile, monochromatic landscapes of *chinoiserie*. Notwithstanding the conspicuously literary flavor of the Jesuit's description, he had at least partially grasped the elements of Chinese garden design, and their expression is implicit, if not explicit, in his account.

Unlike the English gardens, Chinese gardens had, and still have, a deep spiritual significance as havens for contemplation, in which the owner can retire to enjoy the harmony of the two mystical Taoist elements—*yin* and *yang*. In the ideal garden, *yang* (the masculine element: mountains and rocks) and *yin* (the feminine element: water) are perfectly blended.[39] This mystical basis of Chinese landscaping Attiret was doubtless aware of, but he failed to define it, and under his stimulus English gardeners enthusiastically imitated the picturesque Oriental landscapes, unaware of their symbolic design.

The emphasis on Chinese gardens was, during the latter 1750s, so marked, that when Sir William Chambers' *Designs of Chinese Buildings* appeared in 1757, the section on the laying out of gardens attracted far more attention than any

[37]Sir Harry Beaumont [Joseph Spence], *A Particular Account of the Emperor of China's Gardens near Peking*, London, 1752. Large sections of this translation of Attiret's account were reprinted in *London Magazine*, Vol. XXI, 1752; *Monthly Review*, Vol. VII, 1752; *Scots Magazine*, Vol. XIV, 1752.

[38]Dussieux, *Les Artistes français*, pp. 196–99.

[39]Quan, "Chinese Influence upon Eighteenth Century Gardening," Ch. II.

other portion of the book. Though generally considered an ardent Sinophile, Chambers was cool to the prevailing fashions, and one of the purposes of this book was to correct the extravagances of *chinoiserie*. To this end he drew upon the knowledge he had acquired as a supercargo at Canton. Some authentic Chinese designs might offset the excesses of the fashion. Chinese structures he found allowable in palaces or large parks, but he made his position clear: "I am far from desiring to be numbered among the exaggerators of Chinese excellence."[40] He had high praise, however, for the gardens, and this portion of his book, a prologue to the more detailed *Dissertation on Oriental Gardening* (1772), drew much notice.[41]

In it Chambers outlined three types of garden scene sought by the Chinese—the pleasing, the horrid, and the enchanted. In these three types, eagerly copied by English gardeners, lay much of the appeal of the Chinese movement as a whole. The pleasing corresponded, perhaps, to the growing taste for the slowly evolving naturalistic garden. The horrid made the same type of appeal as the flamboyant and emotional Gothic. It opened new vistas in aesthetics. It enlarged the province of beauty. The enchanted set the scene for a restless European society that delighted in the world of illusion, the atmosphere of the masked ball.

By the late 1750s the full force of the Chinese movement in the arts was felt both in England and on the Continent. The gardens of Wilhelmshohe were beautified with a Chinese village and a Negro milkmaid (for want of one of more suitable

[40]William Chambers, *Designs of Chinese Buildings* . . . , London, 1757, Preface. Actually, the opening paragraphs were by Dr. Johnson.

[41]Sections were reprinted in *The Annual Register*, Vol. I, 1758; *The Gentleman's Magazine*, Vol. XXVII, May, 1757; *London Magazine*, Vol. XXVI, May, 1757. See R. C. Bald, "Sir William Chambers and the Chinese Garden," *Journal of the History of Ideas*, XI, No. 3 (June, 1950), 287–320.

complexion).[42] Collectors of virtu, such as Walpole, rejoiced in their China rooms. Orientally styled Gobelins appeared in the great houses. Lolling in gilded Chippendale beds festooned with dragons and lotuses, the aristocracy sipped their morning chocolate or tea, served by diminutive Chinese boys. Whang-At-Ting, the Duke of Dorset's page, was worthy of being twice painted by Reynolds.[43] The debilitating vogue turned robust athletes into fops by producing, the satirists claimed, the male dressing room.[44] The plague even affected the Royal Family. The Duke of Cumberland, commander of Britain's armies, was part owner of the houses where Chelsea china was manufactured and zealously promoted its sales. Near his lodge at Windsor he had a Chinese island, adorned with a house and bridge of Oriental style.[45] Worst of all, he maintained a Chinese yacht, designed by Paul Sandby and trimmed with dragons and lanterns, on which he disported the Royal Family.[46]

The vigor and excesses of the vogue drew the full fire of the satirists. Though these assaults came from many sides, from true-born Englishmen, sour clergymen, and natural malcontents, in the main they came from outraged classicists springing to the defense of Greek and Roman purity.

They focused their attack on one figure especially—the poisoner of the fountainhead of taste, the propagator of the new disease—the virtuoso.[47] In doing so they had ample prece-

[42]Reichwein, *China and Europe*, p. 121.

[43]One of these portraits, currently hanging at Knole, is reproduced both in Victoria Sackville-West's *Knole and the Sackvilles*, London, 1922, and in T. Blake Clark's *Oriental England*, Shanghai, 1939.

[44]*The Connoisseur*, No. 65, April 24, 1775.

[45]Mrs. Caroline Powys, *Passages from the Diary of Mrs. Powys* (London, 1899), p. 114.

[46]Bellamy Gardner, "Duke William's Chinese Yacht," *Connoisseur*, CXXI (March, 1948), 22–25.

[47]Walter E. Houghton, Jr., "The English Virtuoso in the Seventeenth Century," *Journal of the History of Ideas*, III, No. 1 (January, 1942), 51–73; III, No. 2 (April, 1942), 190–219.

dent. Shadwell in his play *The Virtuoso* had sneered at the pseudo-science of Sir Nicholas Gimcrack, and the scientific Sinophile had been laughed at in William King's

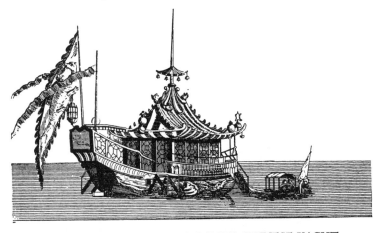

THE DUKE OF CUMBERLAND'S CHINESE YACHT
Paul Sandby, c. 1755
From the Collection of Avery Library

The Transactioneer (1700). An excessive love of rarities and of ludicrously superficial scientific knowledge exposed such dilettantes to ridicule. Typical was King's satire on Sir Hans Sloane's description of the trifling contents of a china cabinet.[48] In a dialogue between a Gentleman and a virtuoso partisan of Sir Hans on the merits of such objects of virtu, the former caustically observed:

Sir, he hath not so much as neglected an ear-picker, or a rusty razor; for he values anything that comes from the Indies or China at a high rate; for, were it but a pebble or cockle-shell from thence, he would soon write a comment upon it, and perpetuate its memory upon a copper-plate.[49]

[48]*Philosophical Transactions of the Royal Society*, XX (1698), 390–92, 461–62.
[49]William King, "The Transactioneer," *Works* (London, 1776), II, 14.

By the mid-eighteenth century, the reputation of the virtuoso had sunk to an even lower level. With Shaftesbury, the
overtones of the word were almost unmitigatedly contemptu-
ous.[50] Level-headed men of common sense such as Dr. Johnson
turned the full fire of their guns on similar lightheaded
amassers of trivia. An essay in *The Rambler* is typical of such
contemporary abuse.[51] In it the Doctor assailed the collector
for coveting such objects as the longest known blade of grass,
or a snail that had inched its way along the Wall of China.
Madness of this order could only end in laughable cabinets of
curiosities and ruined fortunes. Such follies called for severe
indictment, but they came as a consequence of errors in
aesthetics, and these required some analysis.

To this problem of standards the eighteenth century essayists devoted much thought. Addison and Steele pondered the
question and tried to infuse English society with a proper sense
of values, but by the mid-century the need for an aesthetic
touchstone had become intense. What was to guide the man
of culture among the mazes and distractions of the new move-
ments? Although opinions differed, one word cropped up persistently—Taste.[52] But what was it? Aestheticians concentrated
their attention on finding a solution to this question, and
despite the general agreement on the existence of a norm,
they failed to agree on its definition.

John Shebbeare, the satirist, early came to the reluctant
conclusion:

Perhaps there is not a thing upon the face of the earth truer than
the belief that taste is the general possession of all men: I mean

[50]Anthony Ashley Cooper, Earl of Shaftesbury, *Characteristics* (London,
1900), II, 252–55.

[51]*The Rambler*, No. 82, Dec. 29, 1750.

[52]Edward N. Hooker, "The Discussion of Taste from 1750 to 1770, and
the New Trends in Literary Criticism," *PMLA*, XLIX (1934), 577–92;
Robert W. Babcock, "The Idea of Taste in the Eighteenth Century,"
PMLA, L (1935), 922–26.

every man assumes it to himself, tho' he denies it to his neighbor, by which it is at once universal in one view, and non-existent in another.[53]

By and large the aestheticians would have agreed with him. They found it difficult enough to uncover the common denominator of beauty without taking into account the new fashions that complicated its definition. It was therefore only natural for the seekers after true taste, men for the most part with a bias toward classical art, to cry out against the "unnatural" art of Batty Langley's Gothic or Halfpenny's Chinese designs and denounce their works as deviations from Nature and Truth. But even the meaning of the word "nature" was disturbingly ambivalent.[54] To the classicists "nature" suggested, primarily, simplicity and order. To the partisans of the Gothic and Chinese it suggested the asymmetry of these two styles. In the tree-lined walks they found the Gothic arch approximated. In the variety of the world of the out-of-doors they found the irregularity of the Chinese style.[55]

In the clash between the two schools, classic and romantic, symmetric and asymmetric, the final definition of the word remained in doubt. If anything, the tide of public opinion seemed to favor partisans of the Gothic and Chinese, a trend which outraged such conservative critics as John Gilbert Cooper. In his rambles near London he found nothing but architectural evidences of impertinence, unmeaning glitter,

[53]Batista Angeloni [John Shebbeare], *Letters on the English Nation*, 2d ed. (London, 1756), II, 269–70; Letter LVII.

[54]Arthur O. Lovejoy, "Nature as Aesthetic Norm," *Modern Language Notes*, XLII, No. 7 (November, 1927), 444–50; "The First Gothic Revival and the Return to Nature," *Modern Language Notes*, XLVII (1932), 419–46; "The Chinese Origin of a Romanticism," *Journal of English and Germanic Philology*, XXXII (1933), 1–20.

[55]Henry Home, Lord Kames, *Elements of Criticism* (Boston, 1796), II, 353–54. The first edition was published in Edinburgh in 1762.

and the tasteless profusion that sprang from denial of the orderly classic conceptions of beauty.[56]

Joseph Warton shared Cooper's antipathy to these monstrous villas. Like him he sympathized with the doctrines of Shaftesbury who had so clearly developed the relationships between Taste, Nature, and Morality. Judgment was the virtue of a cool and disciplined personality. Taste was the concomitant of this virtue. The immoral pretenders to this fruit of virtue Warton could clearly designate:

. . . what shall we say of the taste and judgment of those who spend their lives and their fortunes in collecting pieces, where neither perspective, nor proportion, nor conformity to nature are observed; I mean the extravagant lovers and purchasers of CHINA, and INDIAN screens. I saw a sensible foreigner astonished at a late auction, with the exorbitant prices given for these SPLENDID DEFORMITIES, as he called them, while an exquisite painting of Guido passed unnoticed, and was set aside as unfashionable lumber. Happy should I think myself to be able to convince the fair connoisseurs that make the greatest part of Mr. Langford's audiences, that no genuine beauty is to be found in whimsical and grotesque figures, the monstrous offspring of wild imagination, undirected by nature and truth.[57]

The shallowness and false nature of this taste the critics of the Chinese vogue constantly emphasized. As true taste had a moral foundation, and a foundation in nature, such deviations found no precedent in morals or nature. "Taste consists in a nice harmony between the fancy and the judgment,"[58] the classicists repeated, allowing at least for a modicum of imagination. But fancy most certainly did not reside in the eccentric caprices of collectors of virtu.

The consequences of such unguided taste, the critics

[56]John Gilbert Cooper, *Letters Concerning Taste*, 4th ed. (London, 1771), p. 57; Letter IX.
[57]*The World*, No. 26. June 28, 1753.
[58]*The Connoisseur*, No. 120. May 13, 1756.

claimed, manifested themselves unmistakably among lovers of *chinoiserie,* particularly among the feminine collectors of porcelain. While Goldsmith laughed generously at their frivolous sense of values,[59] other satirists railed. One maintained that in the event of a French invasion the ladies' primary concern would be for their china.[60] In an amusing imaginary visit to Bedlam with Dean Swift, Joseph Warton described the final consequences of a virtuoso's folly. Among the wreckage of humanity in the madhouse they encountered Lady Harriet Brittle, driven mad by the loss of a favorite mandarin figure, and reduced to so pitiful a condition that she mistook native Chelseaware for true Nankin.[61]

Another victim of the frenzy was the newly rich citizen, determined to indulge in the fashionable excesses. But what was ridiculous on grounds of taste among the upper classes, the satirists found even more ludicrous among the solid citizens. Thus George Colman and Bonnel Thornton satirized Joseph Wilkins of Thames Street, councilman and cheesemonger, who dreamed of a house at St. James's and a Chinese "snugbox" at Hampstead.[62] Similarly, Robert Lloyd in *The Cit's Country Box* laughed at the social aspirations and aesthetic pretensions of a *nouveau riche* couple.

> Blest age! When all men may procure
> The title of a Connoisseur. . . .
> Now bricklayers, carpenters, and joiners,
> With Chinese artists and designers,
> Produce their schemes of alteration,
> To work this wondrous reformation.
> The useful dome, which seeret stood
> Enbosom'd in the yew tree wood,

[59]*The Citizen of the World,* Letter XIV.
[60]*The Connoisseur,* No. 113. March 25, 1756.
[61]*The Adventurer,* No. 109. Nov. 20, 1753.
[62]*The Connoisseur,* No. 93. Nov. 6, 1755.

The trav'ller with amazement sees
A temple, Gothic or Chinese,
With many a bell and tawdry rag on,
And crested with a sprawling dragon.
A wooden arch is bent astride
A ditch of water four feet wide;
With angles, curves, and zigzag lines,
From Halfpenny's exact designs.[63]

Such a "Chinese madness," according to John Gilbert Cooper, seemed to distemper the gentry the moment they left the city air. It was likely to disturb the lives of the most sensible citizens. One such, a wealthy landowner plagued by a fashionable wife in league with an Oriental upholsterer, within a short space of time found his house unrecognizably altered to the prevailing fashion.

There is not a bed, a table, a chair, or even a grate that is not twisted into so many ridiculous and grotesque figures and so decorated with heads, beaks, wings, and claws of birds and beasts, that Milton's "Gorgons, and hydras, and chimaeras dire," are not to be compared with them.[64]

Cursed with such a wife, the solid citizen proved as subject to the inexorable laws of economics as the eccentric virtuoso. While his house became a fashionable show place, the fine rolling acres surrounding it melted away. So persistent was the vogue in spite of these dire financial consequences, that as late as 1779 the essayists in *The Mirror* were still pointing out to citizens similar examples of false taste and bad economy.[65]

From their aesthetic and economic attacks on proponents of the vogue, aristocratic virtuosi and aspiring bourgeois, the es-

[63]Robert Lloyd, "The Cit's Country Box," *The Connoisseur*, No. 135. August 26, 1756.
[64]*The World*, No. 38. Sept. 20, 1753.
[65]*The Mirror*, No. 17. March 23, 1779.

sayists turned to lampooning aspects of *chinoiserie* itself. Primarily they ridiculed fashions in architecture and furnishings. Chinese influences on the landscaping of English gardens they paid less heed to. The reason is not far to seek. The English garden amalgamated many styles during the 1750s, and the exact nature of China's contribution was disputable. Some later writers, such as Gray,[66] Mason,[67] and Richard Cambridge,[68] disclaimed the Chinese influence altogether, and John Shebbeare in his *Letters on the English Nation,* in the chapters on gardens that immediately follow his attack on *chinoiserie* in architecture, nowhere associates the Oriental and Occidental styles.[69]

China's part in garden ornament and architecture was, nevertheless, sometimes lampooned. Essayists laughed at the capricious permutations of classic porticoes into Gothic towers, Lapland houses into Chinese villas, and temples of Venus into Hermitages.[70] Such curious metamorphoses and juxtapositions of pagan and Christian, classic and Oriental, suggested still another line of attack. If these inanities were perpetrated in private and domestic architecture, what consequences might not result in public buildings and places of worship?

In the name of orthodoxy the satirists frowned on the jumble of foreign architectural styles. Westminster Abbey, they feared, might set a new tone by catering architecturally to Egyptian or Mohammedan superstitions, and doubtless the Chinese vogue would soon follow. "And how elegant must a monument appear . . . erected in the Chinese taste, embellished with dragons, bells, pagods, and mandarins."[71] William

[66]Thomas Gray, *Letters,* ed. Duncan Tovey (London, 1912), III, 26–27; to William Taylor Howe, September 10, 1763.

[67]*Ibid.* See William Mason's footnote.

[68]*The World,* No. 118. April 3, 1755.

[69]Shebbeare, *Letters,* Vol. II, Letter LVII.

[70]Richard Owen Cambridge, *The World,* No. 76. June 13, 1754.

[71]*The Connoisseur,* No. 73. June 19, 1755.

Cowper gently gibed at the ruinous expense of indulging tastes for Chinese railings in a poor country parish,[72] and an unknown essayist in *The World* hinted that St. Stephen's was shortly to be fitted out with Chinese benches and an Eastern throne.[73]

Here the classicists most clearly revealed themselves. They saw Palladian pediments and columns transformed into pagodas and minarets and raised outraged cries against such desecration. The greatness of the Grecian was abased to the meanness of Gothic and Chinese. They traced in alarm fluctuations of favor from Greek to Roman to Chinese, from Palmyra and Corregio to corrupt and Gothic design. One essayist in *The World,* however, consoled himself with the reflection that these transient vagaries of taste and this passion for novelty had existed even among the Athenians.

Strange as it may appear that this should find admirers, yet it is not any more to be wondered at than the applause which is fondly given to Chinese decorations, or to the barbarous productions of a Gothic genius, which seems once more to threaten the ruin of that simplicity which distinguished the Greek and Roman arts as eternally superior to those of every other nation.[74]

It was both the strength and the weakness of the British system that it permitted the placement of the mandarin between the busts of Tully and Demosthenes, although as one outraged Athenian declared, "if the same innovating taste should intrude upon the muses' shrine in our public seats of learning, I should wish for some authority to stop so sacrilegious an attempt."[75]

[72]*The Connoisseur,* No. 134. Aug. 19, 1756.
[73]*The World,* No. 59. Feb. 14, 1754.
[74]*The World,* No. 117. March 27, 1755.
[75]*The World,* No. 171. April 8, 1756.

The trend of history, however, played into the hands of the classicists. They had attacked the debasing foreign influences on aesthetic, economic, and pseudo-religious grounds. The events of 1756 furnished them with the still more powerful argument of patriotism. As the downfall of Garrick's *The Chinese Festival* had been largely due to anti-French feeling, so the Seven Years War contributed much to the decline of the vogue for the foreign and exotic. *Chinoiserie* appears to have been regarded as a decadent enemy trait. In *The Apparition; or, Mand'rin's Ghost,* the French king was warned:

> Then kneel no more, but let alone
> Thy monkey gods of wood and stone.[76]

The superiority of British goods was celebrated in *Lines on Seeing an Armed Bust of the King of Prussia on a Porcelain Cup of Worcester Manufacture.*

> Perhaps thy art may trace the circling world,
> Wheree'er thy Britain has her sails unfurl'd:
> While wand'ring China shall with envy see,
> And stoop to borrow her own arts from thee.[77]

By the time of the peace the cult had subsided considerably. Horace Walpole, that arbiter of fashion, makes a significant entry in a letter to George Montagu on September 24, 1762.[78] In it he refers to his conversion of Richard Bateman from the Chinese to the Gothic. The extent of this triumph is evident in a letter of much later date.

I am as proud of such a disciple as having converted Dicky Bateman from a Chinese to a Goth. Though he was the founder of

[76]*The Gentleman's Magazine*, XXVI (1756), 88.
[77]*Ibid.*, XXVII (1757), 564.
[78]Walpole, *Letters*, V, 247, to George Montagu, Sept. 24, 1762.

the Sharawadgi taste in England, I preached so effectively that his every pagoda took the veil.[79]

Although Walpole appears to be exaggerating the importance of his proselytizing (there is no foundation for his claim that Bateman was the founder of this taste), his remarks suggest a point of recession.

Books of Chinese designs nevertheless continued to appear, though in less number than formerly. Among them were a number spawned by Chippendale's *Director*: Thomas Johnson's *One Hundred and Fifty New Designs* (1761), *The Joiner and Cabinet-Maker's Darling* (1770), *The Cabinet and Chair-Maker's Friend* (1775), and William Wrighte's *Grotesque Architecture; or, Rural Amusement* (1767), which followed in the tradition of the Halfpennys. Teahouses still dotted the landscape. Gilded and lacquered furniture still appeared in some drawing rooms and Mrs. Caroline Powys, in the course of her incessant touring, bears ecstatic witness to this continued undercurrent in the tide of taste. She exclaims over "Menagareths" (Chinese bedrooms) and delights in the Eastern furnishings of Rose Hill and Sir Walter Blount's house.[80] *A Peep into the Principal Seats and Gardens in and about Twickenham* (1775) discloses many fashionable houses still Oriental in furnishing. In addition, the public gardens further indicated the survival of this taste after 1760. Vauxhall still fenced off its gardens with Chinese railings; a Chinese temple still decorated the canal at Ranelagh.[81]

Most notable of all were Sir William Chambers' improvements in Kew Gardens. Through the patronage of Augusta, Dowager Princess of Wales, he obtained the commission to landscape the grounds and the opportunity to realize some of the plans projected in his *Designs*. Along with such diverse

[79]*Ibid.*, XII, 10–11; to the Earl of Strafford, June 13, 1781.
[80]*Passages from the Diary of Mrs. Powys*, pp. 63, 114, 123, 139, 148.
[81]Allen, *Tides in English Taste*, II, 178.

buildings as a mosque, a Roman arch of triumph, and several small temples, he erected a pavilion[82] adorned with panels of the life of Confucius and the famous ten-tiered pagoda which was imitated all over Europe.[83] But the Chinese taste was no longer fashionable in England. What had once been novel and esoteric had become *démodé* and public, and Chambers himself bears considerable responsibility for the vogue's decline.

His success at Kew led him to elaborate some of his earlier garden theories into his *Dissertation on Oriental Gardening* (1772). What differentiates them from those expressed in the *Designs* is their lack of moderation. The theories of Attiret and Chambers had been spared during the satirical barrage of the 1750s, when the asymmetry of the Chinese and English gardens seemed to have so much in common. By 1770, however, the tastes of many had shifted. Almost deliberately, it seems, Chambers challenged the rising popularity of the naturalistic school of landscape gardening whose chief advocate, "Capability" Brown, had been preferred over Chambers to lay out the gardens for Clive's villa at Claremont.[84]

Motivated as it may have been, in part, by malice and disappointment, the Chambers' *Dissertation* had at the same time a real aesthetic purpose—to attack the overly "natural" garden which, the author felt, needed the complementing hand of art. In calling attention to Chinese gardening he demonstrated how coherence was achieved by a skillful use of planting and topography and by centering on some focal point. He chose, however, to combine this analysis with some colorful topographic and architectural passages in the vein of the literature

[82]*The Gentleman's Magazine*, XLIII (June, 1773), 281. Chambers' original drawing is now in the Metropolitan Museum of Art.

[83]Chambers' work became well-known through the publication of his *Plans, Elevations, Sections and Perspective Views of the Gardens and Buildings at Kew*, London, 1763.

[84]A. Trystan Edwards, *Sir William Chambers* (London, 1924), p. 21.

of wonder. His description of the Halls of the Moon and his scenes of terror and surprise seem, as Isabel Chase remarks, "to have been his form of Kubla Khan."[85] Chambers himself admitted he was not entirely serious in his purpose, for in a letter to Goldsmith, accompanying the second edition of the *Dissertation* which included Chit-qua's discourse, he remarked, "and if a successful poet can Step down from the Clouds for half an hour to read fifty pages of Sublunary nonsense, I should be very glad to hear his Opinion."[86]

His enemies needed no such prompting. They seized on some of the imaginative passages in which Chambers, citing Chit-qua as his authority, offered examples of the effective superimposing of art upon nature. Many aspects of the English landscape needed but the touch of art, so Chambers suggested, to fulfill their natural possibilities. England's wastes and moors offered a fine case in point. One could so easily imagine them converted into scenes of horror.

On some of them are seen gibbets, with wretches hanging in terrorem upon them; on others, forges, collieries, mines, coal tracts, brick or limekilns . . . the cottagers, with the huts in which they dwell, want no additional touches to indicate their misery: a few uncouth straggling trees, some ruins, caverns, rocks, torrents, abandoned villages, in part consumed by fire, solitary hermitages, and other similar objects, artfully introduced and blended with gloomy plantations, would complete the aspect of desolation, and serve to fill the mind, where there was no possibility of gratifying the senses.[87]

Such passages, whose at least partially playful intent has escaped many critics, precipitated a storm around Chambers.

[85]Isabel Chase, "William Mason and Sir William Chambers' 'Dissertation on Oriental Gardening,'" *JEGP*, XXXV (1936), 517–29.

[86]Quoted in R. W. Seitz, "Goldsmith to Sir William Chambers," *Times Literary Supplement*, Sept. 26, 1936, p. 772.

[87]William Chambers, *A Dissertation on Oriental Gardening*, 2d ed. (London, 1773), p. 131.

It broke in the form of the anonymous *An Heroic Epistle to Sir William Chambers* (1773) which in the course of four years ran through fourteen editions. Though mistakenly attributed by Chambers himself to Christopher Anstey,[88] its author has since been clearly established as William Mason.[89]

Besides his friendship for Brown, whose landscaping theories he had exposed in *The English Garden,* Mason's strong Whig sentiments sharpened his satire. Chambers had recently been appointed Comptroller General to a king whose Tory policies Mason detested, and Chambers' *Dissertation* he used as an excuse for a multifaceted attack.

Disregarding the fact that the Gothicism of his own *English Garden* could quite as easily have been similarly lampooned, Mason gibed at the intentionally fantastic passages in Chambers' work and from this starting point proceeded to make a wholesale attack on the current Tory administration. Unconsciously, perhaps, he adopted Shaftesbury's attitude that perversions of taste such as those exhibited by the King's Comptroller could only result from deeply rooted social and political corruption. Walpole records that George's malicious amusement in pointing out the satire to Chambers turned to rage as he discovered himself to be the principal victim.[90]

The popularity of the poem, in imitation of Pope's satiric couplets, must be attributed primarily to its author's politics. From his censure of George, he turned to the politics of Bute and Mansfield and the objectionable influence of the Scotch at court. By its very diffuseness, however, the poem defeated its object. Mason lashed out in too many directions, and his interpretation of Chambers' work was manifestly unfair.

Chambers' own response was negligible. He made little de-

[88]Seitz, "Goldsmith to Chambers," *TLS* (Sept. 26, 1936), p. 772.
[89]Walpole, *Letters,* VIII, 257; to William Mason, March 27, 1773.
[90]William Mason, *Satirical Poems,* with notes of Horace Walpole, ed. Mrs. Paget Toynbee (Oxford, 1926), pp. 53-54.

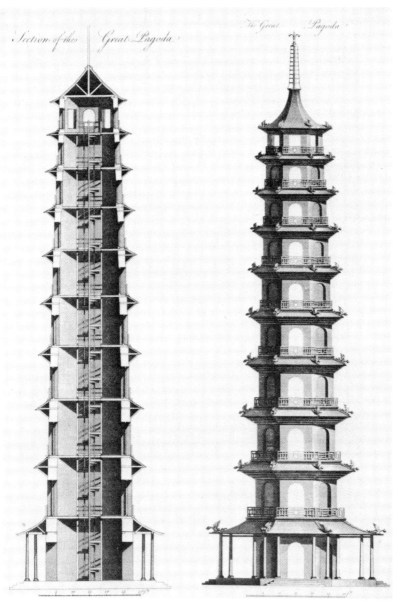

PLANS FOR A CHINESE PAGODA AT KEW
Chambers, 1763
From the collection of Avery Library

LOUM KIQUA
Burford, 1757

fense of his landscaping theories but instead accused his attacker as a false patriot, defacing the royal image.[91] Perhaps he felt disinclined to make a stronger rebuttal. When Goldsmith offered to write a poem in defense of the *Dissertation,* Chambers replied that it was hardly worth while: "Leave my little book to fall or Stand, by its own Strength."[92] Besides, the publicity had sold the remainder of the first edition and, "if I took in hand to laugh at my Self I could do it much better."[93]

Chambers' apathy was justified, for in Mason's *An Heroic Postscript* (1774), a further answer to Chambers, the satire is blunted and the poem comes close to being an apology. Ultimately, it proved hardly necessary to make one. The Chinese phase was a passing one with Chambers, and his later solid achievements, such as the classically designed Somerset House, more than restored his reputation.

This controversy signaled the end of the satiric attacks on *chinoiserie,* save for isolated examples like an essay in *The Lounger* in 1786 which described Lady Bidmore "lost in a chaos of pagodas, wagging-headed mandareens, and bonzes, red lions, golden dogs, and fiery dragons."[94] By the last two decades of the century the vogue had burned itself out, and it was not until the First Gentleman of Europe perpetrated the Oriental pavilion at Brighton that the ghost of *chinoiserie* was again revived.[95]

The fundamental weakness which contributed to its collapse in the eighteenth century is obvious. Primarily the whole movement was a superficial one. Europe was not subjected to

[91]William Chambers, *A Familiar Epistle to the Author of The Heroic Epistle . . . ,* London, 1774.

[92]Seitz, "Goldsmith to Chambers," *TLS* (Sept. 26, 1936), p. 772.

[93]*Ibid.*

[94]*The Lounger,* No. 79. Aug. 5, 1786.

[95]Martin S. Briggs, *Men of Taste* (New York, 1947), pp. 187–88; Margaret Barton and Sir Osbert Sitwell, *Brighton,* London, 1935; Steegman, *The Rule of Taste,* pp. 36–51.

genuine Chinese art or theories. It was subjected to an imitation of China seen through European eyes. Some far-seeing contemporary critics clearly divined this, and the classically minded William Whitehead faced the temporary eclipse of Greece and Rome calmly, confident in the inevitable collapse of this hybrid *chinoiserie.*

. . . not one in a thousand of all the stiles, gates, rails, pales, chairs, temples, chimney-pieces, &c &c &c which are called Chinese, has the least resemblance to anything that China ever saw.[96]

The Gothic movement had similarly collapsed. The spiritual exaltation that had raised the cathedrals of the Middle Ages was unknown to the eighteenth century revivers of medievalism. The spirit that had built Strawberry Hill was no more Gothic than the motivation behind the Pagotenburg or Monbijou was genuinely Chinese. In France, *chinoiserie* coexisted with the rococo till both were swept away by the flames of the Revolution. Fundamentally superficial, neither style could survive alone. In England the superimposing of the Gothic and Chinese during the 1760s and 1770s was far more short-lived. The disastrous wedding of the two styles, each associated with doctrines of asymmetry, accentuated the weaknesses of both. Such freaks of art perish quickly.

The second cause of the decline was the strictly circumscribed knowledge of genuine Chinese art. The Jesuits had suppressed knowledge of the Taoist and Buddhist art which either they aesthetically misunderstood or, for religious reasons, did not wish to interpret, and it was not until the nineteenth century that Europe became aware of the symbolical and mystical aspects of Chinese art.[97]

[96]William Whitehead, *The World,* No. 12. March 22, 1753.
[97]Reichwein, *China and Europe,* has a good account of the limitations of Europe's early knowledge of Chinese art.

Even within the field of non-religious art the Chinese scope was largely confined to flower and bird paintings. Le Comte turned in revulsion from their human representations.[98] Du Halde largely shared his antipathy,[99] and publication of a series of portraits of illustrious Chinese evoked astonishment at the "monsters of deformity, unparalleled in any former exhibition of human nature."[100] A series of engravings of the postures of practitioners of Cong Fou, similar to Yogi exercises, apparently struck reviewers as typically maladroit Chinese figure-drawing.[101] John Shebbeare inveighed against such physical representations which "a prudent nation would prohibit for the sake of pregnant women."[102]

Non-representational techniques likewise baffled the critics.

The paintings, which, like the architecture continually revolt against the truth of things, as little deserve the name of elegant. False lights, false shadows, false perspective and proportions, gay colours, without that gradation of tints, that mutual variety of enlightened and darkened objects, which relieve and give force to each other at the same time that they give repose to the eye, in short every combination of forms in nature, without expression and without meaning, are the essentials of Chinese painting.[103]

Such was the general attitude. Though Temple, Attiret, and Chambers had all shown some sympathy for non-representative and symbolic art, the critics and public remained content with the brilliantly superficial *chinoiserie*. Artists who had an opportunity to study under the Chinese artist Saô, during his

[98]Louis Le Comte, *Memoirs and Observations* . . . , 3d ed. (London, 1699), p. 156.
[99]J. B. Du Halde, *Description* . . . *de la Chine* (Paris, 1735), II, 185.
[100]Article on Vol. III of *Mémoires concernant l'histoire de la Chine*, in *The Monthly Review*, LXIX, Appendix, 1778, p. 521.
[101]Article on Vol. IV of *Mémoires concernant l'histoire de la Chine*, in *The Monthly Review*, LX, Appendix, 1779, p. 551.
[102]Shebbeare, *Letters*, II, 261; Letter LVI.
[103]*The World*, No. 117. March 27, 1755.

stay in Europe, declined to do so.[104] The *rêve chinois* remained a synthetic European product.

Other factors also contributed to the decline during the second half of the eighteenth century.[105] The discovery of the antiquities of Herculaneum, Pompeii, and Palmyra revived interest in the rival field of classical antiquities. Orientalists shifted their attention to concentrate on the rich field of Hindu culture. The noble sage of the antique Chinese civilization gave place to the noble savage of the primitive South Seas. Commercial relations between England and China grew increasingly strained,[106] and native English products increasingly took the place of expensive imports. By the end of the century the piquant figures that tiptoed over delicate landscapes and around exquisitely tinted vases had become symbols of a civilization at once stagnant and tiresome.

[104]Guerin, *La Chinoiserie en Europe*, p. 7.

[105]Allen, *Tides in English Taste*, Vol. II, *passim*.

[106]Earl H. Pritchard, *The Crucial Years of Early Anglo-Chinese Relations, 1750–1800* (Pullman, Washington), IV, Nos. 3–4, September and December 1936.

VII

THE CHINESE
SPECTATOR

*H*E THAT WOULD TRAVEL for the entertainment of others, should remember that the great object of remark is human life,"[1] Dr. Johnson once observed in prescribing the ingredients of a sound travel journal. The exotic novelties of China or Peru held little appeal for him. Certainly they attracted him far less than the proper study of mankind—man himself. Consequently, he felt the need to sift the accumulations of the merchants and missionaries. As an accretive instinct had been at work in the seventeenth century, so in the eighteenth it was necessary to develop a more selective and architectonic one, to appraise customs and manners, not through superficial feelings of pleasure or dislike, astonishment or disdain, but by weighing them against the norm of human life. The arbiter of such a norm was, by implication at least, a citizen of the world, a dispassionate observer capable of detecting subsurface similarities between peoples rather than their dissimilarities.

The ancestry of such a traveler was distinguished. Cicero and Plutarch apostrophized the citizen of the world, and Bacon in his *Essays* remarked:

If a man be gracious and courteous to strangers, it shews he is a citizen of the world and that his heart is no island, cut off from other lands, but a continent that joins them.[2]

Addison echoed this sentiment in the *Spectator*, No. 69. By the mid-eighteenth century the tolerant observer of human

[1] *The Idler*, No. 97, Feb. 23, 1760.
[2] "Of Goodness and Goodness in Nature."

life was so well established a type that Goldsmith in Letter VII of *The Citizen of the World* rejected the ordinary traveler with contempt.

Let European travellers cross seas and deserts merely to measure the height of a mountain, to describe the cataract of a river, or tell the commodities which every country may produce; merchants or geographers, perhaps, may find profit by such discoveries; but what advantage can accrue to a philosopher from such accounts, who is desirous of understanding the human heart, who seeks to know the *men* of every country, who desires to discover those differences which result from climate, religion, education, prejudice, and partiality? . . . How many travellers are there, who confine their relations to such minute and useless particulars! For one who enters into the genius of those nations with whom he has conversed, who discloses their morals, their opinions, the ideas which they entertain of religious worship, the intrigues of their ministers, and their skill in sciences, there are twenty who only mention some idle particulars which can be of no real use to a true philosopher. All their remarks tend neither to make themselves nor others more happy; they no way contribute to control their passions, to bear adversity, to inspire true virtue, or raise a detestation of vice.

But who could qualify as that *rara avis*, the wise traveler, since European voyagers were eliminated? In *The Citizen of the World* Oliver Goldsmith exalted Lien Chi Altangi to that honor, and in a series of letters to his friend Fum Hoam, the wise Chinese anatomized the English scene. His use of the Oriental observer and the pseudo-letter genre was already a well-worn practice.[3]

[3]Hamilton J. Smith, *Oliver Goldsmith's The Citizen of the World*, Yale Studies, No. 71, 1926; Ch'en Shou-yi, "Oliver Goldsmith and His Chinese Letters," *T'ien Hsia Monthly*, VIII (January, 1939), 34–52; Levette J. Davidson, "Forerunners of Goldsmith's Citizen of the World," *Modern Language Notes*, XXXVI, No. 4 (April, 1921), 215–20; Ronald S. Crane and Hamilton J. Smith, "French Influence on Goldsmith's Citizen of the World," *Modern Philology*, XIX, No. 1 (August, 1921), 83–92; Arthur L. Sells, *Les Sources françaises de Goldsmith*, Paris, 1924.

The device of the pseudo-letter from a foreign observer dates as far back as Giovanni Paolo Marana's *Letters Writ by a Turkish Spy* (1687), a series of political satires enclosed within the frame of a story. Pope and Arbuthnot in the concluding Advertisement to the *Memoirs . . . of Martinus Scriblerus* projected a third book describing Martin's voyage with the Bishop of Apamaea "upon Cunturs to China," with an account of its religion and policy, including in addition the journal of a Chinese prince traveling incognito through the courts of Europe.[4] Montesquieu in his *Lettres persanes* (1721) selected two Persians to dissect contemporary French life, and George Lyttelton in *Letters from a Persian in England to His Friend at Ispahan* (1735) similarly analyzed his native land. The Marquis D'Argens in his *Lettres chinoises* (1739) made further use of the genre, identifying his observer with the fashionable Chinese visitors of the period.[5]

The vogue for such literary spectators was established on the Continent largely because of actual visitors who, in addition to their social novelty, had the virtue of seeing Europe through fresh eyes. The Chinese was merely one among a throng of these vaguely delineated commentators, but as the reputation of Confucius soared in Europe, the Chinese visitor inevitably partook of the character of the sage. From the time of Hakluyt and the sixteenth century missionaries the portrait of the scholar-saint had become familiar. The translations of his maxims, the moral tales based upon them, and the vigorous Jesuit propagation of his cult had led to his acceptance as the Socrates or Plato of the East. In spite of the decline of taste for the more extravagant forms of *chinoiserie*, and the sporadic

---

[4] *Memoirs of the Extraordinary Life Works and Discoveries of Martinus Scriblerus*, ed. Charles Kerby-Miller (New Haven, 1950), p. 172.

[5] Goldsmith's debt to D'Argens is discussed in Ch. V of H. J. Smith, *Oliver Goldsmith's The Citizen of the World*. See also Newell R. Bush, Columbia University Dissertation, 1949, "The Philosophical Correspondence of the Marquis D'Argens."

attacks upon the sage by caviling philosophers and divines, he was still generally reverenced. He continued to enjoy more or less the same adulatory biography. The account of the sage in *The Gentleman's Magazine* of 1742, written at the beginning of the Chinese madness, is remarkably similar to that in *Scots Magazine* twenty years later,[6] a date which marked the publication of *The Citizen of the World* and, roughly, the decline of the Chinese movement in the world of art. If anything, the laudatory tone of the biography was heightened in the later account, and though Walpole and the classicists sounded the knell of the Chinese vogue, the House of Confucius triumphantly confronted them at Kew, and the sage continued to be compared very favorably with his near-contemporaries, Pythagoras and Solon. "His philosophy, though sublime, was quite free from those subtile and intricate questions with which that of the best Greek philosophers was clogged."[7]

In his monograph on the "Good Man" of the eighteenth century, Charles Whittuck makes the suggestion that it was precisely this quality, the power of simplifying virtue, which the English valued so highly in the "good man."[8] In contrast, the French and Continental writers leaned toward the sage. The English approach was less intellectual. In the character of Confucius they found an amalgam of the qualities of the good men of the eighteenth century: the detachment and wit of the Spectator, the personal devoutness and purity of William Law, the human compassion and understanding of Parson Adams. The parallels between the state religion of Confucianism and the Deists's ideals are obvious, but the main appeal of Confucius lay in the personality of the man himself. Here indeed was a man who would have been acceptable

[6] Compare the accounts in *The Gentleman's Magazine*, XII (July, 1742), 354–57 and *Scots Magazine*, XXIV (August, 1762), 413–15.

[7] *Scots Magazine*, XXIV, 413.

[8] Charles Whittuck, *The Good Man of the Eighteenth Century* (London, 1901), pp. 181–231.

at almost any English dinner table. In fact, how like an Englishman he was!

Colored in part then by the character of Confucius, Goldsmith's Lien Chi Altangi derived also from actual visitors and from the traditional Chinese spectator used for the medium of political satire. Ever since Sir William Temple and the Jesuits had acclaimed China as a land of philosopher-kings, it had been natural for eighteenth century political pamphleteers to turn to it as a source of contrast to displeasing aspects of English political life. Eustace Budgell's *A Letter to Cleomenes* (1731), an anti-Walpole attack, bristles with invidious comparisons of this sort.

In the Preface to his letter Budgell exposed his unbounded admiration for the Chinese government and its system of competitive examinations for official posts.

Having shown that Real merit is the only Qualification for a Post in China; I beg leave to add that England has always made a figure in Europe, and been more or less Considerable, in proportion as this Maxim was more or less observed by her Princes.[9]

China's freedom of the press, its system of keeping secret and impartial historical records, and its practice of memorializing the Emperor to redress faults of his own or the empire, Budgell contrasted with inferior British practices. How lamentably alien were these fine Chinese precepts must have been made evident to Budgell when he sought to memorialize the King with a petition against Walpole.[10]

His *Letter to His Excellency Mr. Ulrick D'Ypres, Chief Minister to the King of Sparta* (1731), another Walpole satire, was, at any rate, more discreet. Though still intent upon assailing the Whig prime minister, Budgell used a more indirect

[9]*A Letter to Cleomenes* . . . (London, 1731), p. 99.
[10]*A Letter to the Craftsman* (London, 1730), pp. 27–28.

attack by allegorically contrasting the wise Chinese with the decadent Tonquinese.[11] He told the story of an indolent prince of Tonquin and his evil prime minister Xunchi who packs his council with creatures as ignoble as himself. In the face of the gathering storm clouds of public opinion, Budgell related, the evil minister gathered his cabal of hack-writers to abolish freedom of the press and plan his defense. But even political corruption has its limitations. Xunchi's leading apologist confesses that Confucius himself could not defend such corruption, and the guilty statesman, overcome by shame, recognizes the depths of his own degradation. Imploring his agents to keep on drinking, gaming, and whoring, in a burst of honesty, he concludes, "for God's sake don't defend me!"[12]

Such attacks on Walpole's ministry appear to have been numerous during the 1730s and 1740s.[13] Using Chinese maxims and fables, anonymous writers in the *London Journal*, *London Gazeteer*, and *Fog's Journal* attacked and admonished the current administration. Of this type are two miscellaneous essays by Lord Chesterfield.

The first, in *Fog's Journal*, January 24, 1736, Chesterfield devoted to the thesis that human behavior is everywhere similar, dictated by the same pursuit of pleasure and the avoidance of pain. On this theme he developed a playful fable on the Chinese delight in having their ears tickled.[14] He noted the emperor's pleasure in his official ear-tickling by the empress, and her delight in turn with the ear-tickling of an aspiring mandarin. The lesson in government was plain. Flatterers,

[11]*A Letter to His Excellency Mr. Ulrick D'Ypres* . . . (London, 1731), pp. 71–81.

[12]*Ibid.*, p. 87.

[13]Ssu-Yu Teng, "The Chinese Influence on the Western Examination System," *Harvard Journal of Asiatic Studies*, VII (1943), 267–312.

[14]Philip Stanhope, Lord Chesterfield, *Miscellaneous Works* (London, 1778), I, 8–14.

Chesterfield tells us, produced similar vibrations in English ears. The moral for governors was palpable: "Guard your ears, O ye Princes, for your power is lodged in your ears."[15]

In *Common Sense,* May 14, 1737, citing Du Halde, he praised China as an example of morality and good government and related the Chinese fable of the rat gnawing at the innards of a statue.[16] He compared its depradations with those of worthless intruders in the governmental system. Was it not possible to shake the statue and dislodge the rodents, he asked? "But," he concluded with mock bitterness, "is it possible that the useful art of rat-catching should be unknown to so ingenious a people as the Chinese?"[17] *A Letter from an Old Discarded Minister to One Lately Disgraced in China* (1745?) made use of the same thin geographic disguise to preach a similar lesson in practical statesmanship.

Horace Walpole, whose father had been attacked through this medium, himself made use of the convention for satirical political comment. In the enormously popular *A Letter from Xo-Ho, a Chinese Philosopher at London, to His Friend Lien Chi, at Peking* (1757) the Chinese observer analyzed the case of Admiral Byng and the political scandal it had generated.[18] The caprices and prejudices of British political justice are held up to ridicule as the hero, Xo-Ho, ponders the trial, acquittal, and condemnation of Admiral Byng and the trial of his associates to see if they should be returned to office. Such proceedings baffled Walpole's commentator. He could not fathom the relationship of the king to his minister, found the English incomprehensible, and came to the reluctant conclusion, "Alas! alas! dear Lien Chi; England is not China."[19]

[15]*Ibid.,* p. 14.   [16]*Ibid.,* p. 42–46.   [17]*Ibid.,* p. 45.
[18]Horace Walpole, *Works* (London, 1798), I, 205–9.
[19]*Ibid.,* p. 208.

But the Chinese visitor, prior to his appearance in *The Citizen of the World,* had non-political functions as well. He served to illuminate Walpole's satiric essay on scholarship, in which the author foresaw, in an appalling vision, a world entirely covered with books.

I can easily conceive that a Chinese or Indian, hereafter visiting Europe, may acquaint one of his correspondents, in the hyperbolic style of the East. "That it is exceedingly difficult to travel in these countries by reason of vast waste tracts of land, which they call *libraries,* which being very little frequented, and lying uncultivated, occasion a stagnation of bad and unwholesome air; that nevertheless, the inhabitants, so far from destroying or rooting out what they so little either use or esteem, are continually extending these deserts; that even some of the natives, who have waded farther than ordinary into these forests, are fond and proud of transplanting out of one part into another; and though they are sure that their labours will be choked up the next day by some of their neighbours, they go on in their idle toil, and flatter themselves with the hopes of immortality for having contributed to extend a wilderness, into which nobody thinks it worth his while to penetrate."[20]

As a self-appointed inquisitor in a world deluded by pedantry, and misled by the false lights of scholarship, Walpole facetiously traced his ancestry back to Chi Hoang Ti— that "much injured name"—who had ordered the conflagration of China's libraries. Such an ancestor he vigorously defended. Who would not honor such a man? In place of sterile monuments to learning he had left rich rice crops.

In the pleasant *jeu d'esprit, Mi Li,* a Chinese fairy tale, Walpole further exploited this talent for graceful fantasy.[21] Here he introduced still another Chinese traveler, Mi Li, a

[20]*Ibid.,* p. 198.   [21]*Ibid.,* IV, 342–47.

lovelorn prince, seeking his beloved through the fulfillment of a dark prophecy:

> ... he would find his destined spouse, whose father had lost the dominions which had never been his dominions, in a place where there was a bridge over no water, a tomb where nobody ever was buried nor ever would be buried, ruins that were more than they ever had been, a subterraneous passage in which were dogs with eyes of rubies and emeralds, and a more beautiful menagerie of Chinese pheasants than any in his father's extensive garden.[22]

Happily he found these conditions ingeniously fulfilled in the picturesque garden of William Campbell, late governor of Carolina, whose daughter Caroline became, in consequence, the Princess of China.

Such delightful fictional visitors were ancestors to Lien Chi Altangi. They had their counterpart as well, however, in real life. From the time of their first appearance in England and France, at the close of the seventeenth century, Chinese voyagers had been warmly received. Some, it appears, were social pretenders, imposing on a gullible public, and Louis Le Comte records with gusto smoking out such an impostor.[23] In Paris he encountered a lady who had assumed the role of a Chinese princess driven to Europe by a succession of shipwrecks and captivities. From the first the Jesuit father distrusted her story. Chinese ladies do not go on extended voyages. Birth in a palace is unlikely "where there is none but eunuchs." When her audacious attempts to pass off a "wild ridiculous gibberish" as Chinese proved too much for the Jesuit, he unmasked her. Her male counterpart in England had considerably more success. Passing himself off as a Japanese convert to Christianity, George Psalmanazar foisted

[22]*Ibid.*, pp. 344–45.

[23]Louis Le Comte, *Memoirs and Observations* . . . , 3d ed. (London, 1699), pp. 126 ff.

his *Historical and Geographical Description of Formosa, an Island Subject to the Emperor of Japan* (1704) on a public unaware of its fictitious nature and of the fact that the island belonged, indeed, to China. London society lionized him, and he was established in rooms at Oxford to teach a Formosan jabberwocky to the eager scholars there before the immensity of the fraud was revealed.

More genuine visitors, such as the Chinese converts who accompanied Father Couplet on his return trip to Europe in 1685, were also received with acclaim. One of these, Shen Fo Tsung, the guest of Dr. Hyde at Oxford in 1687, attracted the attention of the monarch himself. On a visit to the university, James II catechized Dr. Hyde searchingly on the subject of his visitor.

"Well, Dr. Hyde, was the Chinese here?" To which he answer'd "Yes, if it may please your majesty; and I learned many things of him." Then said his majesty "He was a little blinking fellow, was he not?" To which he answered "Yes," and he added that "all the Chineses, Tartars, and all that part of the world was narrow-eyed."[24]

The learned curator of the Bodleian had indeed been quick to take advantage of his visitor's presence.

Mei in rebus Sinicis Informator fuit D. Shin Fo-Cung, Nativus Chinensis Nakinensis, quem ex China secum adduxerunt R.P.D. Couplet & reliqui fratres Jesuitae qui nuperis annis in Europam redierunt, & Philosophiam Sinicam Parisiis ediderunt. Fuit quidem juvenis xxx.p.m. annos natus, optimae indolis, valde sedulus & studiosus, natura comis, moribusque benignus, per totem vitam in Sinensium Literatura & philosophia educatus, in eorum libris versatissimus, & in lingua Sinica promptissimus: & is unicus ac solus ex Indigenis jam in China superstes aliquid Linguae Latinae callens. Antea fuerat alius quidam, sed tunc defunctus. Natus erat a Christianis parentibus; nam Pater antea a Missionariis fuerat

[24]*Life and Times of Anthony Wood* (Oxford, 1894), III, 236.

conversus. Ab eo linguae Sinicae partem didici, & de multis capitibus scripto excepi informationes, quarum magis particularem mentionem feci post Praefatione, Libri nostri cui Titulus *Itinera Mundi;* ad quem, Lectorem ut de his certior fiat, remitto.

Is omnium Sinicorum Ludorum, qui in hisce Libellis occurrunt, notitiam & descriptionem mihi dedit, & Charactres propria manu descripsit. Fuit enim vir scientae multae & generalis, in omnibus suae patriae rebus optime & critice versatus. Et cum certior factus essem talem hominem Europae rarum appulisse Londinum, illum inde ad Oxonium accersendum curavi, ut ex illius informatione pleniorem de rebus Sinicis notitiam habere possumus.[25]

Shen Fo Tsung's compatriot, Huang, who had also sailed from China with Father Couplet, remained in Paris to work on a Chinese dictionary and was also the center of much attention.[26]

The infrequency of such travelers is evident, however, from the curiosity that they continued to awaken. Visitors from the Orient were still so novel in 1756 that an antiquary, writing to a friend, recorded in detail his meeting with a mandarin.[27] The sole blemish on the occasion was the fact that the stranger spoke only Portuguese. This understandably dashed the learned Englishman's expectations, for the contents of his letter reveal that he associated the Chinese with the descendants of Noah and considered them the likeliest decipherers of Egyptian hieroglyphics. Doubtless he had indulged momentary visions of startling the learned world through the stranger's knowledge. Deficiencies in English were apparently atoned for, however, by social talents. A correspondent in *The Gentleman's Magazine* was so impressed

[25]Thomas Hyde, "Praefatio ad Lectorem," *Mandragorias seu Historia Shahiludi,* Oxford, 1694.

[26]Kenneth Ch'en, "*Hai Lu,* Forerunner of Chinese Travel Accounts of Western Countries," *Monumenta Serica,* VII (1942), 210–11.

[27]John Nichols, *Literary Anecdotes of the Eighteenth Century* (London, 1812–15), IX, 604–5.

by the visitor's lively renditions on a guitar-like instrument that he transcribed in full one of these Chinese airs.[28]

Although he is not mentioned by name in either of these accounts, the stranger was undoubtedly Loum Kiqua, a merchant who had left Canton on a Portuguese ship and had arrived in Lisbon just in time to experience the terrible earthquake of 1755. He had many troubles with the Portuguese and escaped in the next year to England where his fortunes took a turn for the better. The Royal Family received him, the nobility petted him, and his full-length portrait was painted by Daniel Serres.[29] In 1757 he returned to his country on one of the East India Company's ships.

By 1769 when Tan Chitqua, or Chit-qua, a molder of clay busts, arrived in England the Chinese vogue was in its decline. Nonetheless the visitor attracted much interest. He had obtained leave from the Chinese government to visit Batavia but had continued his journey westward on an East Indiaman, induced by "curiosity and respect" to visit England.[30] In one respect, at least, he had the advantage over his predecessors. He spoke some English and a kind of lingua franca. He achieved considerable success in London, and Sir William Chambers in his *Dissertation on Oriental Gardening* has given us a diverting description of him:

All the world knew Chet-qua, and how he was born at Quang-chew-fu, in the fourth moon of the year twenty-eight; also how he was bred a face-maker, and had three wives, two of whom he caressed very much; the third but seldom, for she was a virago and had large feet. He dressed well, often in thick sattin; wore nine whiskers and four long nails, with silk boots, callico breeches and every other ornament that Mandarins are wont to wear; equalling therein the prime macarones, and scavoir vivres, not

[28]*The Gentleman's Magazine*, XXVII (January, 1757), p. 33.
[29]A mezzotint of the Serres portrait was executed by Thomas Burford.
[30]*The Gentleman's Magazine*, XLI (May, 1771), 237–38.

only of Quang-chew, but even of Kyang-ning, or Shun-tien-fu. Of his size; he was a well-spoken portly man, for a Chinese; a pretty general scholar; and, for a heathen, a very compleat gentleman. He composed a tieh-tse, or billet doux, at pleasure; recited verses, either in Mantchou or Chinese, and sang love-songs in many languages. He likewise danced a fandango, after the newest taste of Macao, played divinely upon the bagpipe, and made excellent remarks; which, when he lodged at Mr. Marr's, in the Strand, he would repeat to his friends over a pipe, as often as they pleased; for he was fond of smoaking, provided the tobacco was good; and, upon these occasions, was always vastly pleasant, and very communicative.[31]

Richard Gough, in writing to Benjamin Forster, found the occasion of his meeting with this distinguished Oriental so stimulating a one that he described Chit-qua in detail.[32] Sir William Jones also seems to have had knowledge of his presence in London, for he advised John Wilmot to consult him about some characters which needed deciphering.[33]

During his stay Chit-qua was honored, as Loum Kiqua had been, by an audience with the King and his mother, the former commissioning him to model portraits of the Royal Infantry. Thus auspiciously launched, Chit-qua busied himself with a profitable series of clay busts at ten pounds apiece, and full-length statuettes at fifteen, which were successful enough to impress Josiah Wedgwood's partner, Thomas Bentley.[34] His crowning success came in April of 1770 when

[31]William Chambers, *A Dissertation on Oriental Gardening,* 2d ed. (London, 1773), pp. 115–16. R. C. Bald, "Sir William Chambers and the Chinese Garden," *Journal of the History of Ideas,* XI, No. 3 (June, 1950), 287–320, doubts that Chambers actually knew Chit-qua.

[32]John Nichols, *Illustrations of Literary History of the Eighteenth Century* (London, 1828), V, 318.

[33]Lord Teignmouth, *Memoirs of the Life . . . of Sir William Jones,* 2d ed. (London, 1806), p. 98.

[34]William T. Whitley, *Artists and Their Friends in England, 1700–1799* (London, 1928), I, 269–70.

he attended the first official dinner of the Royal Academy, sharing the limelight with the Duke of Devonshire, the Earl of Carlisle, Garrick, and Walpole. The following year he was included in Zoffany's group-portrait, *The Life School at the Royal Academy*, now in Buckingham Palace.

His experiences were not always as pleasant. During an attempt to return to China in the following year he ran into some unexpected difficulties.[35] His curious dress and appearance alarmed the stolid English mariners on the East-Indiaman which he was to board at Gravesend. When he accidentally fell overboard and was rescued by the superstitious sailors, they wholeheartedly cursed him as a Jonah, and the terrified artist pled with the ship's carpenter to make him a coffin and smuggle his body ashore. The captain facilitated matters by conveying him to land, but once returned to London his confusion and inability to remember his address caused fresh trouble. Safely returned to his lodgings, he sensibly adopted English dress and his subsequent reembarkation on an East India Company ship was without incident. The last mention of him is an almost affectionate one in T. J. Mathias' *Imperial Epistle from Kien Long*, where he is recalled as Chet-qua, "admired by beau and belle, Chet-qua, whom all the world knew passing well."[36]

Apparently the face-maker also retained affectionate memories of England, for shortly after his return, inspired by his example, another Chinese appeared on the English scene. In *The Bee* of September 12, 1792, in a letter dated February 18, 1775, "by a gentleman who is now no more," this subsequent visitor is described.

I have lately met in company Whang-At-Ting, the Chinese, who is now in London; of whom, if you have not received any

[35]*The Gentleman's Magazine*, XLI (May, 1771), 237–38.
[36]Thomas J. Mathias, *The Imperial Epistle from Kien Long* . . . (London, 1795), ll. 281–82.

account, you may perhaps like to hear some particulars. He is a young man of twenty-two, and an inhabitant of Canton, where having received from Chitqua, the Chinese figure-maker, a favourable account of his reception in England, two or three years ago, he determined to make the voyage likewise, partly from curiosity, and a desire of improving himself in science, and partly with a view of procuring some advantages in trade, in which he and his elder brother are engaged.[37]

The author was, almost undoubtedly, Sir Joshua Reynolds, who died in February, 1792. He had painted the Chinese youth's portrait twice.[38] In a letter written to Sir William Jones many years after his London stay, the Oriental visitor recalled with pleasure the kindness of his English friends, and mentioned in particular dining with Sir Joshua Reynolds and Mr. Blake.[39] Though the identity of the latter is not certain, in all probability Whang-At-Ting referred to the father of John Bradby Blake, a supercargo of the East India Company and a distinguished amateur naturalist, who died in Canton in 1773.[40] Not improbably Blake had been acquainted with the young Chinese there, and that his London career should have begun under the aegis of Mr. Blake's father is not unnatural. Besides making the acquaintance of Jones and Reynolds, Whang-At-Ting also met Thomas Percy who, in his diary for March, 1775, recorded spending a morning at Mr. Blake's examining some Chinese drawings and conversing with the Oriental visitor.[41] Most important of all, Whang-At-Ting was introduced to the Duke of Dorset who took him

[37]The Bee, XI, Sept. 12, 1792.

[38]Sir Walter Armstrong, Sir Joshua Reynolds (London, 1900), p. 235.

[39]Sir William Jones, Works (London, 1801), Supplemental Vol. I, pp. 245–46.

[40]The Annual Register, XVIII (1775), 31–35.

[41]Quoted by Ch'en Shou-yi, "Thomas Percy and His Chinese Studies," Chinese Social and Political Science Review, XX, No. 2 (July, 1936), 224.

into the household at Knole, where the visitor's portrait still hangs, and arranged for his education at Sevenoaks.[42]

But despite these social successes, Whang-At-Ting's stay was apparently a short one. He returned to his business at Canton, and, though Sir William Jones corresponded with him briefly on a proposed translation of the odes of *Shih-Ching*, there is no evidence that any part of this proposed work was completed.[43]

Similar visitors on the Continent likewise attracted attention. In 1732 a Chinese theological college had been established in Naples for those Orientals selected by the Jesuits for theological and philosophical studies. One of them, Louis Fan, became a Jesuit.[44] Two others, Kao Lei-ssu and Yang-Te-wang, who were sent to France, met a gratifying welcome and spent some thirteen years there. They, also, had come as theological students, but they had so startled their instructors with their progress in studies and with the breadth of their knowledge, that they were commissioned by the French to submit a series of papers on various aspects of China. Their correspondence with Poivre after their return had a profound influence in shaping the theories of the physiocrats.[45]

Exactly at what point this procession of strangers first suggested to Goldsmith the creation of Lien Chi Altangi it is difficult to say. He was well aware of the Chinese rage of the early 1750s, but he was far from succumbing to it. Rather, it had induced in him a playful mockery. While still a literary

[42]Victoria Sackville-West, *Knole and the Sackvilles* (London, 1922), p. 192.

[43]Jones, *Works*, I, 372.

[44]Louis Pfister, *Notices biographiques et bibliographiques sur les Jesuites de l'ancienne mission de Chine 1552–1773* (Shanghai, 1932–34), II, 664–65.

[45]Lewis A. Maverick, "Chinese Influences upon the Physiocrats," *Economic History*, III, Nos. 13–15 (February, 1938), 54–67; "The Chinese and the Physiocrats: a Supplement," *Economic History*, IV, No. 15 (February, 1940), 312–18.

unknown, in August of 1758 he had evoked a pleasing vision of the future reception of his works in China, when an Oriental scholar would note:

Oliver Goldsmith flourished in the eighteenth and nineteenth centuries. He lived to be an hundred and three years old . . . age may be justly styled the sun of . . . and the Confucius of Europe . . . learned world, were anonymous, and have probably been lost, because united with those of others. The first avowed piece the world has of his is entitled an "Essay on the Present State of Taste and Literature in Europe"—a work well worth its weight in diamonds. In this he profoundly explains what learning is, and what learning is not. In this he proves that blockheads are not men of wit, and yet that men of wit are actually blockheads.[46]

That Goldsmith was acquainted to some extent with French Sinology before 1760 is evident from his review in March, 1759, of Goguet's *De l'origine des lois,* and soon after of Murphy's adaptation of Voltaire's play, *L'Orphelin de la Chine.*[47] His approach to China in this second review was again a casual one. With the attitude of tolerant amusement, he applauded Murphy for altering and exploiting Voltaire's version. Though Goldsmith had the gift of detecting trends and adapting them to his own advantage, he remained curiously aloof from such fluctuations of taste as his essay on *The Instability of Worldly Grandeur* humorously indicates.

A Chinese who had long studied the works of Confucius, who knew the characters of fourteen thousand words, and could read a great part of every book that came in his way, once took it into his head to travel into Europe and observe the customs of a people whom he thought not very much inferior even to his own countrymen in the arts of refining upon every pleasure. Upon his arrival at Amsterdam, his passion for letters naturally led him to a bookseller's shop; and as he could speak but little Dutch, he civilly

[46]Goldsmith, *Works,* ed. Peter Cunningham (Boston, 1900), VIII, 238.
[47]*Ibid.,* VII, 247–51, 253–60.

asked the bookseller for the works of the immortal Ilixofou. The bookseller assured him that he had never heard the book mentioned before. "What, have you never heard of that immortal poet," returned the other, much surprised, "that light of the eyes, that favorite of kings, that rose of perfection! I suppose you know nothing of the immortal Fipsihihi, second cousin to the moon?" "Nothing at all, indeed, sir," returned the other. "Alas!" cries our traveller, "to what purpose then has one of these fasted to death, and the other offered himself up as a sacrifice to the Tartarean enemy, to gain a renown which has never travelled beyond the precincts of China!"[48]

When Goldsmith first cogitated a series of "foreign spy" letters, so Prior tells us, he contemplated making his spectator a citizen of Morocco or Fez, but decided instead to take advantage of the prevailing fashions and make use of a Chinese spectator.[49] The idea that "Un Asiatique qui voyagerait en Europe pourrait bien nous prendre pour des païens," irresistibly appealed to him.[50] It offered to him, as it had to Montesquieu, opportunities for ingenuity and paradox. In addition, it lent a fashionable edge to his delicate thrusts at society. His initial *Chinese Letter* appeared in *The Public Ledger* on January 12, 1760, and during the next twenty-two months two letters a week ensued. So popular were they that they were soon given space in the first column, and were reprinted in other journals and periodicals.

It was their style and wit, however, rather than their Chinese flavoring, which accounted for their popularity. Goldsmith had made use of Le Comte and Du Halde, but for their materials alone. Their air of panegyric is absent. Had his examination of English society been more slashing, more doctrinaire, he might, for purposes of contrast, have measured

[48]*Ibid.*, V, 106–7.

[49]Sir James Prior, *Life of Goldsmith* (London, 1837), I, 360.

[50]Voltaire, "Dictionnaire philosophique," *Oeuvres* (Paris, 1877–85), XVIII, 255.

English beliefs and manners against those of an alien civilization. But Goldsmith was content with a less trenchant analysis, pricking absurdities and follies as his predecessors Addison and Steele had done. Though he at first tried with some seriousness to pose as a genuine philosophical traveler, the role did not become him. The consciously exalted tone of the first few letters, thought befitting a Chinese visitor, soon subsided to a less extravagant key. Goldsmith's effervescent, convivial personality could not long remain hidden behind the robes of the learned mandarin. Beau Tibbs and the Man in Black were more to his taste. There was no need, after all, to retain his disguise. His attention was centered on English foibles and manners. His commentator merely needed, like the four Indian kings, the advantage of fresh vision. The direct statement of such a visitor proved more effective than interminable evaluations against a remote culture. Since the human heart was both the subject and the instrument of the analysis, the question of nationality and idiom was of small importance. In no sense was Goldsmith a fervent Sinophile. Rather he was a temperate cosmopolitan, echoing the dictum of Montesquieu: "Le coeur est citoyen de tous les pays."

VIII

THE TIDE

RECEDES

$\mathcal{T}$HE CHINESE VOGUE among English literary men culminates nominally in Goldsmith's *Chinese Letters*, but in 1762 it was already in a decline. When the letters were collected for publication, Goldsmith significantly altered their title to *The Citizen of the World*. So slack was the demand for the book that a second edition did not appear until 1769. Poivre's French translation, on the other hand, had considerable acclaim and ran through seven editions by 1766. What was eagerly devoured on one side of the Channel had become increasingly less palatable on the other.

In Thomas Percy's works dealing with China the drift in taste was even more marked.[1] Far more at home as a Sinologist than Goldsmith, his distrust of the Chinese legend was evident in his version of *Hau Kiou Choaan* (1761),[2] a Chinese novel which he found partially translated by his friend Captain Wilkinson, who had studied Chinese with a Portuguese tutor. With his searching mind and tireless interest in varied cultures, Percy seized upon this tale.[3] The section in Portuguese which the Captain had not transcribed he himself translated, and, after polishing the whole, he circulated it among the publishing houses. The most interesting feature of the cor-

[1]Ch'en Shou-yi, "Thomas Percy and His Chinese Studies," *Chinese Social and Political Science Review*, XX, No. 2 (July, 1936), 202–30.

[2]*Hau Kiou Choaan; or, The Pleasing History*, 4 vols., London, 1761.

[3]Percy's use of this manuscript has been much discussed. See Vincent H. Ogburn, "The Wilkinson MSS and Percy's Chinese Books," *Review of English Studies*, IX, No. 33 (January, 1933), 30–36; L. F. Powell, "Hau Kiou Choaan," *Review of English Studies*, II, No. 8 (October, 1926), 446–55.

respondence between Percy, Grainger, and Shenstone as to the fate of this manuscript is its slow transformation from a Chinese novel to a "Europeanized" one. Sensing the shifts in the tides of taste, publishers expressed a wary interest that suggested to Grainger, who was acting as Percy's intermediary, the advisability of Anglicizing the heroine. When the translator finally adopted the suggestion, Grainger professed himself delighted with the heroine's "new English garb."[4] Percy was less sanguine; his expectations were as mixed as the emotions he felt toward the characters of the novel.

Hau Kiou Choaan, the first Chinese novel to be translated into English, tells the story of Shue-ping-sin, a rich heiress, and her uncle's efforts to force her into an unwanted marriage. A woman of exceptional resource, the slant-eyed Clarissa Harlowe escapes one pitfall after another, but her greatest task lies in soothing the excessively tender scruples of her lover, Tieh-chung-u, an Oriental Sir Charles Grandison.[5] Three volumes later the lovers emerge unscathed and united from a plot complicated by abduction, poisoning, rape, and rebellion, to win a royal citation for transcendent virtue.

The translator, while he displayed considerable admiration for his wily heroine, also revealed a subtle hostility to the Chinese in general. Grasping magistrates, corrupt officials, and absurd attention to ceremony determine the convolutions of the plot, and Percy's copious footnotes, many of a hostile nature, punctuate the narrative throughout. Their tone is as scholarly as it is antagonistic, for the translator relied on many sources for his information, and his books of reference, listed in the first volume of the translation, read like an

[4]John Nichols, *Illustrations of Literary History of the Eighteenth Century* (London, 1848), VII, 261.

[5]L. Carrington Goodrich, *A Short History of the Chinese People* (New York, 1943), p. 226 refers to a Chinese novel by Ts'ao Hsueh-ch'in (1719–64) as comparable in emotional effect to the novels of Richardson.

eighteenth century bibliography of China. He relied largely, however, on Du Halde's compilation of missionary accounts for his textual comment and for the selections of Chinese verse and apothegms with which he rounded out his work.[6]

The question of his debt to Goldsmith is a debatable one.[7] There is little doubt that Goldsmith's story of the Chinese matron inspired the Percy version of the same tale, and, conversely, that the framework story of Percy's translation may have suggested in part the plot structure of *The Citizen of the World*. Percy's interest was, however, that of the scholar rather than the casual essayist or satirist, and his background studies for *Hau Kiou Choaan* are almost certainly the source of his *Miscellaneous Pieces Relating to the Chinese* (1762), compiled largely from the Jesuit narratives. But his interest in the subject was, in the final analysis, only transient. Primarily, the patterns of world culture absorbed him, and from a study of Chinese civilization he passed on to more comprehensive labors on northern antiquities. The dubious success of *Hau Kiou Choaan* may well have influenced him in this respect, for though his translation enjoyed subsequent French, Dutch, and German versions, it made little stir in England.[8]

Ange de Goudar's *L'Espion chinois; ou, L'Envoye secret de la cour de Pekin pour examiner l'état present de l'Europe* made still less impression. First published in six volumes in Cologne in 1764, the English translation appeared in Dublin two years later. The flimsiest of framework stories encloses a series of letters from two mandarins-at-large surveying

[6]Tsen Chung Fan, "Percy and Du Haldè," *Review of English Studies*, XXI, No. 84 (October, 1945), 326–29.

[7]Ada Milner-Barry, "A Note on the Early Literary Relations of Oliver Goldsmith and Thomas Percy," *Review of English Studies*, II, No. 5 (January, 1926), 51–61.

[8]For a review of *Hau Kiou Choaan* see *The Monthly Review*, XXV (December, 1761), 427–36.

Europe. So slight is the pretense of nationality, however, that by comparison Goldsmith's letters seem thoroughly Chinese. Occasional allusions to pagodas and mandarins are not enough to disguise the essentially French character of both Chem-pi-pi and Ni-ou-san. In fact, the disguise is so thin that at times they are mistaken by other characters for Frenchmen. Like Goldsmith, De Goudar almost never judges by supposedly Chinese standards. He weighs one European country against another, favoring the French, yet aware at the same time that even England has some advantages which France does not possess.

In Volumes IV, V, and VI he writes of England, and satiric comment is intermingled with a sketchy history of the period when the Seven Years' War was drawing to a close. The specific mention of English theatrical performances and politics suggests a personal knowledge of contemporary England. Indeed, parts of the book, such as the description of Bath, seem designed almost as a guide. The manners and customs satirized are essentially the same as those laughed at in Goldsmith, though without the latter's delicacy and wit.

Occasionally De Goudar manages to achieve some satire that is not cumbrous, as in his description of the English Sinophile.[9] In this pleasant essay he tells of a gentleman's plans for a Chinese newspaper in London, *The Pekin Daily Advertiser.* Although this would-be journalist knows no Oriental correspondents, and though even the professors of Chinese at Oxford know none of the language, such trivialities fail to deter him from his purpose. London must be told how often the Emperor sneezes, how often he takes tobacco, and what the dimensions of his parasol are.

Monsieur D'Alenzon's *The Bonze; or, Chinese Anchorite,*[10]

[9] *L'Espion Chinois* (Cologne, 1764), IV, Letter 43.
[10] D'Alenzon, *The Bonze; or Chinese Anchorite* (London, 1768), 2 vols.

an Oriental epic in two volumes, marks still another stage in the recession. Ostensibly a study of the origin of evil, a problem never satisfactorily resolved by the author, the novel consists of a series of transmigration stories told by one Confuciango. Pseudo-Chinese in setting, the narrative ingenuously juxtaposes an account of the fall of the Ming dynasty, a synopsis of *Paradise Lost,* and a series of erotically tinged adventures in a seraglio. These are knotted together by the curiously named English-speaking *raconteur* who accounts for his fluency in that tongue as a happy result of his conversion by English missionaries. Confucius, or Confuciango, the wisest of the sages, had succumbed to the blandishments of the Church of England!

Though Lien Chi Altangi's followers appear briefly in essays of the 1760s and 1770s, their appearances are ephemeral. An itinerant Chinese philosopher is appealed to in *The Political Controversy,*[11] but the opposing *North Briton* challenges his qualifications as a wise and impartial observer.[12] The decline in his fortunes is further evidenced in Charles Johnstone's *The Pilgrim; or, A Picture of Life* (1775).[13] Its hero, Choang, is a still more attenuated shade of the Citizen of the World, and to bolster his satiric observations on English politics, religion, and manners, Johnstone was forced to graft onto his story a series of tearful digressions. The narratives of harassed heroines and unjustly imprisoned heroes constantly interrupt the progress of the novel, and the blunt and wandering satire is brought to a close only when the death of the pilgrim's wife enforces the end of his critical tour. The anonymous *Oriental Chronicles of the Times* (1785?),[14] "supposed to have been written in the spirit of prophecy

[11]*The Political Controversy,* Sept. 18, 1762.

[12]*Ibid.,* Oct. 16, 1762.

[13]Charles Johnstone, *The Pilgrim; or, A Picture of Life,* London, 1775.

[14]Anonymous, *The Oriental Chronicles of the Times,* London, n.d.

by Confucius," makes use of the clairvoyant sage's observations to castigate the opponents of Charles James Fox. Similarly, Ely Bates's *A Chinese Fragment* (1786)[15] arraigns English immorality and the insufficiencies of English clergymen through the agency of an itinerant Chinese, strongly attracted to the teachings of Jesus.

The career of the Chinese spectator was virtually over. By the 1770s he had lost much of his novelty. The myth of his superiority of manners and morals was dying. To be sure, some still protested that the removal of a Chinese family to England would seem like a transition from a civilized society to a "confusion of savages,"[16] but such comments became increasingly rare.[17]

Popular interest had waned; the earlier panegyric and opprobrium ultimately bored and confused the public. Knowledge of the real China must have seemed almost hopelessly clouded. Most important of all, the suppression of the Jesuits in 1773 robbed China of its best apologists. Soon after, the publication of the laudatory *Lettres édifiantes et curieuses*[18] ceased, and scientists and scholars set themselves to the task of unraveling the tangled web of myth and fact.

The estimate which they made of China was no more flattering than that of the fictional writers. Astronomers continued to probe Chinese chronology and assailed Voltaire for his notion that their annals were beyond dispute. Eclipses such as the one calculated in 2155 B.C. continued to be feverishly computed and discussed.[19] Historians revived the long

---

[15]Ely Bates, *A Chinese Fragment*, London, 1786.

[16]*The Gentleman's Magazine*, XL (February, 1770), 68–69.

[17]*The Quarterly Review*, XIII (April, 1815), 63, contains a scathing portrait of an imaginary Chinese visitor.

[18]*Lettres édifiantes et curieuses des missions etrangères*, Paris, 1702–76, 34 vols.

[19]*The Gentleman's Magazine*, XXVIII (1758), 58–60, 512–13. There are a great number of articles on Chinese astronomy and chronology. See

smoldering debates over the relative antiquity of Chaldean, Egyptian, and Chinese annals. In the light of current knowledge they sought to reintegrate seventeenth century cosmologies and assign China her proper place in the family of nations. These were not, of course, the first such attempts. Bacon and Temple had at least verbally linked China and Peru,[20] and scholars had long sought vainly to correlate Egyptian and Chinese hieroglyphics. Mid-eighteenth century French scholars revived these efforts.

Foremost among these Orientalists was Joseph de Guignes, curator of the French Royal Collection of Oriental manuscripts, and one-time pupil of the scholar Fourmont, who compiled the first French-Chinese dictionary. From prolonged historical study of the Turks and Huns, De Guignes turned to China to appraise its history and culture on a comparative basis. The result was a series of monographs well known both in England and in France.

Though varied in content, all pivoted on his effort to assign China her proper place among world cultures and to assess her cultural debts and benefactions. De Guignes debated, as Bacon had, the possibilities of navigation eastward from China.[21] He cited an ancient Japanese chart known to Sir Hans Sloane, which indicated the possibility of a Chinese migration to Japan, thence across the Bering Straits to Alaska and down the American coastline. (Perhaps he had heard of the presence of Chinese in Mexico City, where they had been imported by the Spaniards from the Philippines

---

Philosophical Transactions of the Royal Society, XXXVI (September and October, 1730), 397–424; XLIV (March, April, and May, 1747), 476–92. *The Monthly Review*, LV (1776), 530–40; LXII (1780), 505–11; I, n. s. (1790), 525–26.

[20]R. G. Howarth, "China to Peru," *Notes and Queries*, CLXXXVII (1944), 188–89.

[21]*The Gentleman's Magazine*, XXIII (1753), 607–8; *The Monthly Review*, XXIX (1763), 517–18.

in the first decade of the seventeenth century.) Boldly developing this hypothesis, he further suggested that the Chinese had also crossed the Pacific by a more southerly route, moving from one chain of islands to another, as far as South America, and that the inhabitants of climes as remote as Tierra del Fuego were in actuality none other than the descendants of wandering Koreans. China had, in short, perhaps endowed the American cultures. But a disquieting question suggested itself. Had China inherited its own culture from elsewhere?

In 1759 he proposed an answer to this question in an essay designed to prove that the Chinese were an Egyptian colony.[22] The thesis was not, to be sure, a revolutionary one. The Royal Society in 1686 had pondered the calligraphy of both nations,[23] and Egypt had long been revered as the cradle of civilizations. The belief persisted that in a hidden valley one might still find the customs of the age of gold observed and probe the secrets of the origin of mankind. Legends of a lost Utopia among the sands of Africa had enlivened such earlier books as Simon Berington's *Adventures of Signor Gaudentio di Lucca* (1746)[24] and the Abbé Terrasson's *Sethos* (Paris, 1731).[25]

De Guignes's theories, much as they may have been stimulated by these imaginative ventures, in all probability received their original impetus from the researches of Huet and, in particular, the Abbé Jean Barthelemy's curious memoir on Phoenician letters.[26] In it the Abbé described his find of a

[22]*The Gentleman's Magazine*, XXIX (1759), 463–66; *The Annual Register*, III (1760), 150–54.

[23]*Philosophical Transactions*, XVI (March-April, 1686), 64–65.

[24]*The Adventures of Signor Gaudentio di Lucca* (Philadelphia, 1799), pp. 130–31.

[25]*The Life of Sethos, Taken from Private Memoirs of the Ancient Egyptians*, 2 vols., London, 1732.

[26]*Réflexions sur quelques monumens phéniciens* . . . , Paris, 1758.

strange Maltese tablet engraved with a Phoenician inscription so strikingly similar to Chinese calligraphy as to convince the learned divine of the derivation of the Eastern characters from this Mediterranean source. Taking his cue from this memoir, De Guignes analyzed Chinese characters into 214 radicals and contended that he found the three Egyptian methods of writing (the hieroglyphic, alphabetical, and symbolic) all paralleled in the Chinese.[27] He found evidence that the Chinese knew alphabetic letters and that their characters were merely monograms derived from the Egyptian. Furthermore, his researches appeared to indicate that the names of the early emperors of Cathay, Yu and Ki, were none other than those of Menes and Athoes, the Egyptian kings. To back this ingenious claim, De Guignes cited historical evidence of the arrival of an Egyptian colony in the Far East some time after the reign of Menes.

Such a thesis, had it been accepted, would have sounded the death knell to all claims of Chinese anteriority, but the evidence was hardly convincing enough to dispose of the problem once and for all. Another fellow student of Fourmont's, Michel Ange Deshauterayes, professor of Arabic and Oriental languages, challenged the thesis with a series of stinging questions.[28] If such a cultural relationship existed, he asked, why then were hieroglyphics common in China yet reserved for the priestly caste in Egypt? Why were no traces of the Egyptian language or religion found in China? Why did the Egyptian princes who emigrated to China fail to retain their Egyptian names? Why was metempsychosis, the doctrine of the Egyptians, not known in China until A.D. 65? Un-

[27]*The Gentleman's Magazine*, XXIX (1759), 464–66; *The Annual Register*, III (1760), 150–54.

[28]*The Gentleman's Magazine*, XXX (1760), 12–15; *The Annual Register*, III (1760), 154–59.

deterred, still another French scholar reiterated De Guignes's argument, citing the Egyptian and Chinese hatred of novelty, their reverence for authority, love of science, hieroglyphical writing, and mysterious physiognomy as incontrovertible proofs of the similarity of origin.[29]

Curious and exotic as these arguments may seem, they were not limited to a circle of French Oriental scholars happily disputing among themselves. The reverberations of the dispute reached England, where both De Guignes's essay and Deshauterayes' objections received airing and paved the way for Tuberville Needham's strange tract, *De Inscriptione quadam Aegyptiaca Taurini Inventa*, published in Rome in 1761.[30] The English scientist focused the attention of scholars on a black marble bust in the King's Museum at Turin. The cabalistic characters engraved thereon had excited his attention, and he had persuaded a native of Peking, then resident at the Vatican, to examine them. Consultation with a K'ang Hsi dictionary, so Needham affirmed, proved them ancient Chinese characters, closely related to Egyptian hieroglyphics. Another round of the quarrel had begun.

The renewal of this controversy between impassioned antiquarians provoked Goldsmith's laughter,[31] and though the debate was confined to a limited number of scientists, by 1764 the issue was still provocative enough to interest members of the Royal Society.[32] In a series of twenty-seven plates they compared ancient and modern Chinese characters with Egyptian hieroglyphics. They called attention to two letters from Edward Wortley Montagu addressed to the Earl of Maccles-

[29]*The Gentleman's Magazine,* XXXVI (1766), 129–32; *Scots Magazine,* XXVIII (1766), 130–32.

[30]*The Annual Register,* V (1762), 128–32; VII (1764), 153–54. *The Monthly Review,* XXIX (1763), 31–34.

[31]*The Citizen of the World,* Letter LXXXIX.

[32]*Philosophical Transactions,* LIX (1764), 489–504.

field, then president of the Society.[33] Comparing the bust with
Needham's plate of characters, Montagu found them dis-
similar, and made the still more surprising discovery that the
marble of the bust matched that quarried near Turin. His
second letter further invalidated Needham's argument. In
this he cited the Abbé Winkelman and the Abbé Bartoli,
antiquarian to the king of Turin, as corroborating his darkest
suspicions of imposture. Still another Italian Oriental scholar
dismissed the characters as mere astronomical signs, and
De Guignes himself, doubtless reluctantly, repudiated Needham's findings as a fraud, and the translation by the Chinese
scholar as mere invention.

Before finally disposing of the matter the Royal Society
dispatched a letter to the Jesuit order in Peking. Although
only a portion of their reply exists, it is an interesting one,
for in it the Jesuit correspondent reviewed the whole problem
of Chinese calligraphy and reported in detail the stupefaction
of the Chinese savants confronted with the inscription.[34]
Some characters, they found, bore a faint resemblance to those
in Chinese dictionaries, but even these could not be connected
into meaningful passages, and the scholars were forced to
conclude the inscription was indecipherable. That it had
puzzled many was no surprise, the correspondent remarked,
for since the days of the Greeks and Romans scholars had
proved incapable of unraveling the enigma of calligraphy.
Questions of cultural relationship were still dangerous quag-
mires, the Jesuit obviously felt, and the troublesome problem
of primacy he diplomatically sidestepped by vaguely suggesting that both China and Egypt had a common derivation in
some antediluvian world.

The problem thus remained unresolved. Nor was the pur-

[33]*Ibid.*, pp. 490–91. See also *The Annual Register*, V (1762), 128–32;
The Monthly Review, XXIX (1763), 34–36.

[34]*Philosophical Transactions*, LIX (1764), 489–504.

pose of Needham's apparent imposture ever satisfactorily
fathomed. Did he merely hanker for controversy with the
learned jackals? Or, as a Catholic, had he attempted to dis-
countenance the die-hard worshippers of the Chinese who
still saw in their civilization the fountainhead of government,
science, and morality?

Though the extent of China's cultural relationship to Egypt
was never satisfactorily established, its reputation was as
tarnished as that of a harassed patrician, accused of imposture
and debt. The jury of scholars continued to bicker, and so
low had China sunk in the opinion of many that Cornelius
De Pauw scornfully rejected De Guignes's theory in view of
the abysmal disparity between the Mediterranean and Asiatic
cultures.[35] If China's culture had indeed some remote Western
origins, it was so contemptible an alliance no self-respecting
Egyptian would acknowledge it.

During the latter half of the eighteenth century, China's
religion provoked much suspicion and distrust, and the outcry
against the Jesuit panegyrics grew steadily in volume until the
dissolution of the order. John de Mosheim in his *Authentic
Memoirs of the Christian Church in China* (1749) inveighed
against their effusions and the consequent dangers to the
Christian faith.[36] *The London Magazine* and *Le Journal Britannique* trumpeted charges of Jesuit distortion, exaggeration,
and omission,[37] and a correspondent in *The Gentleman's
Magazine* provoked a lively controversy by identifying China
with the anti-Christ of Revelations 12.[38] Such thoughtful

[35] *The Monthly Review*, LXII (1780), 521–26; *Scots Magazine*, XXXI
(1773), 704. Daniel Webb's *Selections from M. Pauw*, Bath, 1795, also
promoted these theories.

[36] *Authentic Memoirs of the Christian Church in China* (London, 1750),
pp. 5–6.

[37] *The London Magazine*, XIX (1750), 599; *Le Journal Britannique*, IV
(1751), 77–80.

[38] *The Gentleman's Magazine*, XXV (1755), 9–10, 71–72, 116–17.

churchmen as John Wesley, troubled by the favorable opinions of the Chinese still entertained by Raynal, recognized in him a more dangerous adversary than Voltaire:

Is not the whole labored panegyric . . . a blow at the root of Christianity, insinuating all along that there are no Christians in the world so virtuous as these heathens?[39]

Similarly, when the section on religion in the monumental *Mémoires concernant l'histoire . . . des Chinois* (1776–1814) was reviewed in England, a rigidly orthodox critic warned his readers: "The Deist would do well to eye with attention this hideous picture of religious opinions undirected by the light of divine revelation."[40]

Though this warning was directed chiefly at overzealous partisans of Confucius, it was also aimed at those who were turning their attention to the philosophies of Fo (Buddha) and Lao-Tse. Until the third quarter of the century these beliefs had attracted little notice, since the philosophies did not complement Christian doctrine as readily as Confucianism. The Jesuit commentators dismissed the Taoists and Buddhists as idolatrous minorities, scorned by the enlightened Confucians, and for almost a century it had been impossible to examine their mystical doctrines apart from the grotesque decorations with which they had been encumbered.

When Europeans discovered that not an ignorant minority but a sizable fraction of the Chinese population accepted these beliefs, China's reputation sank still lower. As the underbrush of superstition and fantasy was cleared away, and as the true nature of the beliefs began to emerge, the contempt did not lessen. Religions which had been confused and unsavory in the Jesuit accounts were hardly less so when

[39] John Wesley, *Journal* (London, 1909–16), VI, 187.
[40] *The Monthly Review*, LV (1777), 536.

explained by scholars of comparative religion. De Guignes's explanation of the Taoist doctrine was a case in point.[41] His account was clear enough in describing its derivation from Pythagoras and the Egyptians (the source also of Confucianism). While he described its slow degradation by an ignorant populace into a study of magic and alchemy and into a search for the mysterious beverage of immortality it was still easy to follow him. When, however, he began to analyze its metaphysics he became, to most readers, almost totally incomprehensible.

The heavens arrive at unity by purity,—the earth arrives at unity by tranquillity—the mind arrives at unity by intelligence,—the void (vacuum) arrives at unity by plenitude,—things arrive at unity by production—sovereigns arrive at unity by justice: if things are not so, continues Lao-Tse, (resuming all the links of this series) all must be destroyed.[42]

Revelations of these higher transcendental beliefs left English reviewers gasping at "such effusions of nonsense as surpass perhaps the most extravagant ravings that ever were heard in the cells of Bedlam."[43]

Further accounts by De Guignes of the introduction of Buddhism from India into China created still further antagonism.[44] The fault lay partially in his own uncertainty over the points of difference between Buddhism and Taoism, partly in the fact that the contemplative and mystical ideal appalled Englishmen in general. The prospect of nine years' meditation of "we know not what" made them gasp.[45] So long was it, indeed, before this repugnance was overcome, that even Marshman's

[41]"An Historical Essay Concerning the Study of Philosophy among the Ancient Inhabitants of China," *The Monthly Review*, LVIII (1778), 535–39.

[42]*Ibid.*, p. 539.   [43]*Ibid.*, p. 538.

[44]*The Monthly Review*, LXIV (1781), 548–53.

[45]*Ibid.*, p. 551.

nineteenth century edition of Confucius referred in somewhat condescending terms to the doctrines of Buddha and Lao-Tse.

Little by little China lost her prestige in religion and ethics. Confucius was no longer the sole arbiter of Chinese morals, but co-regent with the despicable Fo and Lao-Tse. The eclipse of China's reputation in other respects was as marked, and even the foremost English Sinologist of the period failed to come to the rescue.

Though Sir William Jones (1746–94) was the next real Chinese scholar after Thomas Hyde, his knowledge was hardly greater than that of his seventeenth century predecessor.[46] In comparison with his studies in Hebrew, Arabic, Persian, and Sanskrit, his knowledge of Chinese was tertiary, and despite his deep and genuine interest in China, and his proposal, shortly before his death, to make a voyage there, his Seventh Anniversary Address to the Asiatic Society in 1790 revealed how muddled and second-hand most of his opinions of that country were.[47] In it he developed vague parallels between the religions of India and China, puzzlingly identifying Fohi (Fu Hsi) with Buddha. He concluded by leaving ethnic questions and problems of comparative religion as tangled as he had found them. Though expressing reverence for Confucius and the book of *Shi-Ching,* of which he projected a translation,[48] his opinions of China were, on the whole, marked by the hostility typical of this later period:

. . . their letters, if we may so call them, are merely the symbols of ideas; their popular religion was imported from India in an age comparatively modern; and their philosophy seems yet in so rude

[46]Tsen Chung Fan, "Sir William Jones' Chinese Studies," *Review of English Studies,* XXII, No. 88 (October, 1946), 304–14.

[47]Jones, *Works,* ed. Lord Teignmouth (London, 1807), III, 137–61; *The Monthly Review,* VIII, n. s. (1792), pp. 495–501.

[48]"On the Second Classical Book of the Chinese," *Works,* IV, 114–25.

a state, as hardly to deserve the appellation; they have no ancient monuments, from which their origin can be traced even by plausible conjecture; their sciences are wholly exotick; and their mechanical arts have nothing in them characteristick of a particular family; nothing, which any set of men, in a country so highly favoured by nature, might not have discovered and improved.[49]

While the sun of China's favor had set, its fading splendors continued to exercise an incurable fascination over some. William Beckford, in the course of his travels in Europe, constantly dreamed of more distant scenes and delighted in tracing imaginary correspondences between the neat landscapes of The Hague and those of Canton or Ning-Po.[50] The panorama of receding Venice reminded him of the Oriental screens and panels he cherished, and gliding down the waterways he fingered the long-stemmed water lilies and speculated on the Tao beverage of immortality.[51]

The passage of the years did not deaden his interest. On a later visit to the Portuguese monastery of Alcobaca he was feasted on birds' nests and sharks' fins, "dressed after the latest mode of Macao," and retiring to the shade of the gnarled orange-trees, the first brought to Europe, he questioned his hosts about the country to which so many of them had once gone as missionaries.[52] They spun tales of artificial gardens and mechanical marvels that would have delighted Mandeville. So the banter went on, around the marble basin in the cloister. But Beckford was behind the times. He was returning in spirit to a China that no longer existed, to the Cathay of the medieval travelers. The Grand Prior of the monastery was of a more modern turn of mind. When the talk turned to the

[49]Ibid., III, 147.

[50]William Beckford, The Travel Diaries, ed. Guy Chapman (Cambridge, 1928), I, 16.

[51]Ibid., pp. 110–11.   [52]Ibid., II, 265–67.

Emperor's belief in himself as the incarnation of the god Fo, he put an end to the chatter and heathen impiety. The shadows had lengthened in the cloister, and gravely he called them inside. It was time for Mass and prayers for the conversion of the Emperor.

IX

THE MACARTNEY

EMBASSY

*A*s CULTURAL RELATIONS. between England and China worsened during the latter portion of the eighteenth century, commercial friction between them increased. The earliest trade missions projected by Elizabeth had been total failures. The later expeditions of Captain Weddell and Captain Dampier had not bettered relations. The third notable English voyage to China was hardly more successful. It brought into increasing focus the sharp disparity between the Jesuit estimates of the Chinese and those of hardheaded Englishmen.

It was in 1743 that Captain George Anson touched briefly and unhappily on Portuguese-held Macao, outside Canton.[1] The occasion was a dramatic one. His ship had cruised halfway around the world. England was at war with Spain and the tides of battle had drawn Anson to the Far East in search of the legendary Spanish treasure ship that trafficked between Acapulco and Manila. When his own ship arrived in Macao it was badly in need of overhauling; his crew, largely made up of aged pensioners impressed from a Chelsea hospital, was in a state of exhaustion, and Anson himself in no mood to tolerate the interminable ritual which governed the Chinese port authorities. He smarted under the contempt of arrogant

[1] George Anson, *A Voyage Round the World in the Years 1740–44*, compiled by Richard Walter, 3d ed. (London, 1748), pp. 469 ff. See also Maurice Collis, *The Great Within* (London, 1942), pp. 219–59; Captain Walter V. Anson, *The Life of Admiral Lord Anson* (London, 1912), pp. 54 ff.

mandarins who were openly anxious to be rid of the trouble-some foreigners as soon as possible, and he found the Chinese port workers grudging and incompetent in carrying out the necessary repairs. A wave of relief swept both the English and Chinese when the *Centurion* was finally refitted and hoisted sail.

But the uncomfortable visitation was not yet over.[2] Once outside Macao, Anson altered his ostensible course to Batavia, and headed instead toward Cape Espiritu Santo in the Philip-pines, where he hoped to intercept the Spanish ship. There for three weeks the English lurked, ceaselessly practicing gun-nery and small arms fire. When the great Spanish galleon, sinking under bullion and treasure, came over the horizon, the English man-of-war fell upon her. Her superiority in man-power and arms was unavailing against Anson's piratical attack, and after a six-hour engagement, the Spanish colors were hauled down. Nearly a month later, with the equivalent of a million pounds in booty, the jubilant English returned to Macao with their prize in tow.[3] They terrified the neutral Chinese with requests for equipment and food, and a series of negotiations with greedy and corrupt officials began all over again. Only after Anson's men had obliged the authorities by quelling a fire raging in Canton were the English requests fulfilled. Only then was the *Centurion* hesitantly allowed to depart. To the end the dignitaries persisted in the *punctilio* and ceremony that so exasperated Anson. As the *Centurion* passed for the last time through the fortified section of the port, the English noticed armed soldiers patroling the parapets. What the telescope revealed seemed symbolic. The stalwart warriors were clad not in hammered steel, but in dazzling silver paper.[4]

[2] The second part of this episode is related in Anson, *A Voyage Round the World*, pp. 510–48.
[3] The Spanish prize ship was sold in Macao. *Ibid.*, p. 546.
[4] *Ibid.*, p. 540.

As if to rend the fabric of the legend still further, Anson concluded his account of China with a discouraging appraisal of its literature, history, and art. Even its much-vaunted government he attacked as weak, dilatory, and venal.[5] The fact that he had visited only one Chinese port did not deter him, and though his contacts had been limited to a small number of officials and port laborers, many Englishmen were apparently ready to accept his categorical opinions. Tired of the Jesuit panegyrics, they seemed almost eager to believe the worst. As one periodical writer remarked:

But tho' the Chinese are inferior to the Europeans in genius, yet may they possibly surpass them in virtue; and this is asserted by the missionaries: But the experience of the English contradicts these amplified notions of the equity, wisdom and power of this nation. They make their whole deportment to be one affected formality, with continual constraint upon themselves, to keep their passions from breaking out in their looks. But can these passions be said to be less real, from being concealed? And may not this very composedness, which they affect, occasion that timorousness, dissimulation, and deceit so general among the Chinese?[6]

Anson's unflattering estimate could not, however, any more than could Defoe's, blacken China's reputation overnight. When his account appeared the vogue for *chinoiserie* still fevered fashionable England, and his damaging remarks were buried in the matrix of a copious narrative. The hostility of Anson had, nevertheless, a slow, pervasive effect. Within eighteen years, fifteen editions of his account had appeared, large selections had been reprinted in periodicals,[7] and it had per-

---

[5]*Ibid.*, pp. 544–46.
[6]*The Gentleman's Magazine*, XX (March, 1750), 116.
[7]*The Universal Magazine* (1748), *Scots Magazine* (1749), and *The Gentleman's Magazine* (1749–50) all ran copious extracts from the account.

meated through the English countryside to such quiet hearths as those of William Cowper and the Unwins.[8] In Europe his narrative achieved sufficient renown for Voltaire himself vainly to attempt a refutation of some of its anti-Chinese sentiments.[9] Later accounts of China corroborated the Englishman's feelings, and in the voyages of Lord Macartney and Lord Amherst the skepticism and irritation of Anson were to deepen into hatred and disgust.

By 1755 the control over foreign ships in the Middle Kingdom had been established.[10] The Hong merchants in Canton had a monopoly on trade, and their stranglehold tightened despite the efforts of the supercargoes of the East India Company. Pleas and appeals to the Emperor merely produced a more restrictive and increasingly legalized system of control designed to guarantee the flow of all merchandise through the hands of the small cabal of Cantonese merchants. This strait-jacketing of trade exasperated the company officials, who were used to more liberal procedures and who were irritated by the patronizing manner of the Chinese magistrates. As members of the literati, the mandarins looked down on the merchants with patrician scorn. As apostles of Adam Smith, the British traders felt an equal disdain. But behind this natural class antipathy there were several specific causes for friction between the two groups. Primarily, the Chinese did not favor the expansion of trade. They looked upon the British as troublesome intruders in the most civilized country on earth. English conceptions of justice were also distinctly at variance with the Chinese. Increasing legal clashes made evi-

[8]See Cowper's poem *The Castaway*.

[9]Voltaire, *Precis du siècle de Louis XV*, Ch. XXVII, in *Oeuvres* (Paris, 1878–85), XV, 317–18.

[10]Earl H. Pritchard, *The Crucial Years of Early Anglo-Chinese Relations, 1750–1800* (Pullman, Washington, 1936), pp. 126–27; Hosea B. Morse, *The Chronicles of the East India Company Trading to China* (Oxford, 1926), I, 297; V, 21–31, 36–44.

dent the fact that the judicial procedures of the Old Bailey were not paralleled in the Cantonese courts. Perhaps the whole problem hinged on the disinclination of the Chinese to deal with the British barbarians on even terms.[11]

The fundamental cleavage between the two groups is corroborated in the accounts of contemporary voyagers. When William Hickey, then a nineteen-year-old cadet, arrived at Macao in 1769 on the East Indiaman *Plassey*, his immediate impression was one of poverty, misery, and corruption.[12] He noted with distaste the women who offered to board the boat and accommodate the sailors, and the avaricious port officials—"Money seems to be the idol they all worship."[13] Although the comforts of the English factory and the companionship of Bob Potts, the fourteen-year-old commander of the *Cruttenden,* served to relieve the strain, Hickey's diary is a record of constant friction between the English and Chinese. The crew of the *Granby,* refusing to submit to Hoppo port inspection, unceremoniously pitched the officials overboard, one of whom was reported drowned. During the subsequent inquiry, eight English sailors mysteriously died. A European surgeon's report that the bodies showed no symptoms of poison quieted a revengeful crew and caused the Chinese to drop their prosecution, but the memory of the incident rankled on both sides. The violation of a strict factory prohibition against women residents was atoned for only by payment of a substantial fine. Minor sources of friction were as abundant. Bob Potts' high-spirited custom of disposing of the tea equipage by flinging it down the stairs or out the window cannot have endeared him to the native servants. When the Englishmen, in

[11]Pritchard, *The Crucial Years,* pp. 107–11.

[12]*Memoirs of William Hickey,* ed. Alfred Spencer, 3d ed. (London, 1919), I, 196 ff.

[13]*Ibid.,* p. 198.

defiance of orders, went through the gates into Canton, they were pelted with dirt and filth. Hickey's memories of a happy stay were largely dictated by the hospitality shown him by his fellow Englishmen in exile.

Ten years later, the *Resolution* and *Discovery*, on their way home after the death of Captain Cook in Hawaii, made a stopover at Macao.[14] Again, there were multiple sources of irritation. The port officials demurred at allowing the officers of the *ladrone* (pirate ship) to visit Canton. The barter for the English ship's cargo of furs was unusually sharp. Few friendships and social ties linked the English and Chinese, Captain King observed, and at his departure he noted that European factories were subject to so many impositions that they might be forced to close up altogether.[15]

Toward the end of the century so critical had these problems become that an embassy direct to the Emperor seemed the only solution. Trade between 1770 and 1780, while it had continued uninterrupted,[16] had remained virtually static in tonnage, enormous as its potentialities were. The Commutation Act of 1784, lowering the tax on tea, and ostensibly wiping out smuggling of that high-priced commodity, in actuality gave English traders an opportunity to corner the European market, and for five or six years after its passage trade spurted sharply.[17] But the directors of the East India Company who held a monopoly on this highly lucrative enterprise, saw in the restrictions imposed by the Hong merchants a hindrance to still greater trade and greater profits. A forthright embassy could clarify misunderstandings. Hence in 1787 Henry Dundas, head of the Board of Control, nominated for the position Lieutenant Colonel Charles Cathcart, an experi-

---

[14]James King, *A Voyage to the Pacific Ocean* (London, 1784), III, 419 ff.
[15]*Ibid.*, p. 424.   [16]Pritchard, *The Crucial Years*, p. 145.
[17]*Ibid.*, pp. 146–51.

enced officer in the Bengal army.[18] The purpose of the mission was outlined to him most specifically. He was to stress the mutual benefits of trade between the nations, plead for a small tract of ground to serve as a depot and trading post, and, in the third place, emphasize the purely commercial nature of the English proposals.

Since a mission of this kind was without precedent, save for the abortive and forgotten Elizabethan ventures, the embassy was painstakingly planned. A variety of expensive presents and an impressive retinue were assembled. When at length on December 21, 1787, the *Vestal* set sail, the future seemed hopeful. From the start, however, disaster haunted the expedition. Storms and sickness plagued the ship on the long voyage to Cape Town. On the second stage of the journey the newly appointed ambassador fell ill and died. The event threw his retinue into consternation, for no successor had been appointed, and reluctantly they turned back to England. On October 8, 1788, they arrived home, after a voyage marked by further calamities.

The necessity for the embassy was so pressing, however, that before long renewed projects were in operation. For this second venture the Board of Control chose George Lord Macartney, a seasoned diplomat who had tested his mettle in Russia, Ireland, and the West Indies.[19] His personal attributes were considerable, and his experience as Governor of Madras a distinct advantage, as the East India Company's trade between India and China at this period was of increasing importance. Nevertheless, Macartney approached his task with the greatest caution. Sir George Staunton, a lifelong friend, he appointed secretary, and from the undersecretaries, scientists, artificers, and musicians to the small troop of accompanying

[18]Morse, *Chronicles*, II, 151–71; Pritchard, *The Crucial Years*, pp. 236–71.

[19]Helen H. Robbins, *Our First Ambassador to China*, London, 1908.

light infantry, the mission was fastidiously selected. Macartney's objectives were those of his unfortunate predecessor, though stipulated in still greater detail. They were: the abolition of extortions, reduction or abolition of export and import duties, a trade depot, the opening of new ports, a different standard of justice, and the encouragement of British manufactures.[20]

Such objectives, though pleasing to the industrialists of England, particularly the owners of the greatly expanded woolen and cloth businesses who were greedily eyeing the prospective new markets, were nevertheless not altogether agreeable to the stockowners in the East India Company. They had preserved a profitable monopoly on this trade since 1600, and such a mission, though it might have the effect of freeing the Company from its bondage to the Hong merchants, might also open up the field for competitors. America was viewing the China trade with increasing interest. The effect of the Commutation Act was not forgotten by European traders, and before Macartney's departure a whispering campaign had already begun in the East. *Agents provocateurs* were quick to point out that under the sober guise of the ambassador of mercantile good-will the imperial British lion lurked.

Even among Englishmen some misgivings dampened the high expectancy. Peter Pindar, the perennial malcontent, gibed bitterly at the preparations for the embassy. He found the presents designed for the Emperor laughably modest and the predatory ambitions of the English patently obvious. His invocation to Macartney and his ship was hardly encouraging:

> Lord! Couldst thou send the Chinese Empire o'er,
> So hungry we should gape for more:
> Yes, couldst thou pack the Chinese Empire up,
> We'd make no more on't than a China Cup;

[20]Pritchard, *The Crucial Years*, pp. 307–11; Morse, *Chronicles*, II, 214-15.

Even then my Lady Schwellenberg would bawl,
"Gote dem de shabby fellows: vat, dis all?" . . .
Then load away with rarities the ship,
And let us cry, "She made a *handsome trip.*"[21]

His Preface to *A Pair of Lyric Epistles,* prophesying the direct outcome of the embassy, closed on an equally gloomy note of apology:

. . . the horrid picture of the future disappointment of our Ambassador and his Suite at Pekin, with the disgracefully attendant circumstances, we hope to be merely a playful sketch of fancy of the Muse; and that she has really been visited by no such flogging illuminations.[22]

The author was more of a Cassandra than he dreamed. Even before the *Lion* left Spithead in September of 1792, the clashing interests of the European, English, and American merchants, and the cool indifference of the Chinese spelled failure for the mission. Nevertheless, the embassy hopefully set sail westward, cruised down the South American coastline, and across the Pacific to Macao.[23] The ceremonious welcome accorded them there and the triumphant progress to Tung-chow buoyed their hopes of success. The ambassador's spirits were further bolstered by the agreeable intelligence that two palaces had been prepared for his residence, one in Peking, and one at Yuan-ming-Yuan. As the inland voyage began, up the waterways toward the imperial city and on to the pavilions of the summer residence, the prospect seemed encouraging. There was only one ominous note. The banners which waved

[21]Ode V of *Odes to Kien Long.* Peter Pindar, *Works* (London, 1812), III, 163–64.

[22]*Ibid.,* p. 122.

[23]The story of this embassy is told in Morse, *Chronicles,* II, 213–54; Pritchard, *The Crucial Years,* pp. 272–384; Collis, *The Great Within,* pp. 260–301. Robbins, *Our First Ambassador,* pp. 180–392, reprints Macartney's own journal. There are in addition many accounts by other members of the embassy.

over the entourage disturbed Macartney deeply. They bore upon them the bold legend: "The Ambassador bearing tribute from the King of England." Nettled as he was at this indignity, he dared take no offense. The slight was in no sense an individual one. From time immemorial China's foreign relations had been conducted in tributary fashion;[24] she had met ambassadors as a sovereign greets a vassal. An objection on Macartney's part might have fatally endangered the whole of his mission, and instead of protesting he chose the wiser course of feigning to ignore it. Upon his arrival at the summer palace of Yuan-ming-Yuan, however, he found himself faced with a still more awkward question of protocol. At the audience with the Emperor it was traditionally expected of foreign delegates that they perform the kowtow. Unprotesting as he had been under the tributary banners, this request exacerbated the English ambassador, who foresaw the possible failure of his embassy because of this preliminary act of submission. It would be well-nigh impossible under such circumstances to negotiate for trade on a free and equal basis. Consequently he proposed an alternative. He agreed to perform the kowtow on the condition that a mandarin of equal rank kowtow to a portrait of George III. This counteroffer was coldly rejected, but ultimately both parties reached a distasteful compromise. The ambassador agreed to kneel upon one knee and bow low.

So masterfully ambiguous was this obeisance at the dawn audience that opinion divided as to whether or not he had actually performed the kowtow. At all events, the occasion passed off without incident. Subsequent meetings were as amiable, but whenever Macartney tried to direct the conversation toward the purpose of his mission, his efforts were skillfully parried. When the summer drew to a close the embassy removed with the court to the winter palace at Peking

[24] J. K. Fairbank, "Tributary Trade and China's Relations with the West," *Far Eastern Quarterly*, I, No. 2 (February, 1942), 129–49.

where the futile comedy continued. The complimentary letter of request from George III produced no results. The painful silence on trade negotiations was broken only when the dis-

RECEPTION OF LORD MACARTNEY AND HIS SUITE AT THE COURT OF PEKING

Gillray, 1792

tracted ambassador hinted broadly that the mission was drawing to a close. Only then was the imperial reply made known, and it was a crushing one. All the requests of the English king were refused in an edict so patronizing in tone it was hardly calculated to alleviate the humiliation of the embassy:

Convinced of the Rectitude of your Intentions, O King, I commanded my Grandees to introduce your Ambassador to me and I received him at my Table. I delivered to him also my Letters for you, together with costly and magnificent Presents for your

Majesty. . . . In the meantime, O King, your Ambassador has requested my minister, to lay before me some Proposals relating to the Trade of Your subjects. . . . Let us however examine this Business impartially,—Your Merchants, and those of all the European Kingdoms who trade to China, have been used for a time immemorial, to repair for that Purpose to Canton. The productions of our Empire are manifold, and in great Abundance; nor do we stand in the least Need of the Produce of other Countries.[25]

Nothing could have seemed more crushing or more final.

In view of such an answer, the continuing attention paid the embassy puzzled Macartney. The English statesman had never before encountered a diplomacy which simulated affection and delusively treated inferiors as equals. As the English made their way southward to Macao once again, their journey seemed so much more a triumph than a rout, that the ambassador took renewed heart. By the time they reached Canton he felt sufficiently revived to confront the viceroy with a detailed list of English complaints and requests. The viceroy's favorable response to some of these requests further encouraged him, and when the *Lion* unfurled her sails for the return trip, Macartney could feel with some justification that the mission had not been a total loss. It had failed to open further trading ports and relax restrictions, but Macartney had at least obtained some minor concessions at Canton, and he had perhaps paved the way for more successful embassies in the future.[26]

The Chinese, on the other hand, can have felt little of this optimism. Their empire was self-sufficient. Their traditions clashed with those of the red barbarians. Even the mechanical products of the West which had so dazzled and amused the late Ming and early Manchu emperors no longer stirred

[25]Morse, *Chronicles*, II, 248.
[26]Pritchard, *The Crucial Years*, pp. 362 ff.

curiosity. The skilled machinist and the artificer capable of scientific demonstrations who had accompanied the embassy had not even been called upon to demonstrate their skill. The strong intellectual curiosity which had stirred the mandarins in the early days of the Jesuits appeared to have evaporated. The embassy had, however, revived British interest, if we are to judge by the stream of narratives published by members of Macartney's entourage after their return.[27] In view of the copious earlier accounts, such a spate of publications hardly seems justified. It was due, doubtless, to curiosity about the true nature of China, which had been so acclaimed and reviled. These British travelers had not merely been transient visitors as Dampier and Anson had been. They had voyaged many miles and seen not only the lowly port life, but the highest court ceremonials as well. With them a reassessment of China could begin. The observation by a reviewer of Sir George Staunton's book to the effect that China was so little known that the slightest information about it was valuable,[28] though it would have come as a distinct shock to Père Du Halde, DeMailla, and the editors of the *Lettres édifiantes*, had, nevertheless, considerable validity. How was one to evaluate the earlier mass of confused and contradictory estimates?

Contemporary eyewitness accounts by Englishmen were, consequently, welcomed.[29] They were not perhaps entirely stripped of the absurdities of the missionary narratives, as

[27]The most notable of these is Sir George Staunton's *An Authentic Account of an Embassy from the King of Great Britain to the Emperor of China*, 2 vols., London, 1797, with a folio of plates by the embassy artist, William Alexander. Aeneas Anderson's *A Narrative of the British Embassy to China, in the Years 1792, 1793, and 1794* was published in 1795 in London, Basle, and Philadelphia.

[28]*The Monthly Magazine*, IV (1797), 508.

[29]*The Annual Register, Anti-Jacobin Review, The British Critic, The Gentleman's Magazine, The Monthly Magazine, The Monthly Review, Scots Magazine* all carry lengthy accounts and selections from Staunton's and Anderson's narratives and also from the notoriously inaccurate *Travels in China . . .*, London, 1804, by John Barrow.

William Winterbotham claimed,[30] but they at least portrayed China as John Bull saw it. Varied as is the material of the narrators, they have at least one feature in common—a subsurface hostility. They did not dare to castigate China too thoroughly, lest they invalidate what little success the mission had and endanger the prospects of a second one. On the other hand, they felt the need to express their resentment.

Sir George Staunton's *An Authentic Account of an Embassy* (1797), the last of consequence to appear, is, on the whole, fairly representative both in tone and material. Though more sympathetic than most to China (his young son, later one of England's first real Sinologists, startled the aging Emperor by prattling to him in Chinese), he was nevertheless dispassionate in his estimate. Infected perhaps by physiocratic theories, he lauded the peasant's devotion to the land and the government's reverence for agriculture. But in most respects he aligned himself with a then-forgotten generation of travelers. His none-too-flattering summary of China's religions, his temperate praise for the tax system, the historical register and competitive civil service examinations, approximate the remarks of the early sixteenth and seventeenth century voyagers. (Accounts by lesser members of the expedition, such as Aeneas Anderson, resembled those of still earlier travelers in their zestful descriptions of *curiosa* and *admiranda*.)

Doubtful as Sir George Staunton, Lord Macartney, and John Barrow may have been as to the over-all success of the embassy, their countrymen had far more decided opinions. In his *Ode to the Lion, Ship of War upon Her Return*, Peter Pindar once more dipped his pen in venom.

> Tell me, *who* planned this silly expedition?
> That brain was surely in a mad condition:
> Say, was it Avarice, the lean old jade,

[30]*An Historical, Geographical, and Philosophical View of the Chinese Empire*, London, 1795, prefatory advertisement.

Who, though half Asia's Gems her Corpse illume
(Sol's radiance on a melancholy tomb),
Can join with Meanness in her dirtiest trade?

Who told our King the Embassy would thrive,
Must be the most egregious fool alive:
God mend that courtier's head, or rather trash-pot!
Perhaps he cried, "Upon the rich Hindoo
Your glorious Majesty has cast its shoe;
And China next, my Liege, must be your wash-pot."[31]

A correspondent in *The Gentleman's Magazine*, nettled by the indignities endured by the British, satirically commented:

Of the propositions tendered by Lord Macartney to this sulky court, and which were all rejected, did ever one stipulate for the residence of British women in the factory that was to be established, or were the settlers to profess celibacy? The use of chintzes, china, and tea should be discontinued by females of all ranks in every part of Europe till this monarch of the Tartar race shall have taken off the embargo on them.[32]

The general indignity was not lessened by the pessimistic reports of mounting difficulties in Canton. The codes regulating foreign trade became increasingly stringent, and the treatment of foreigners increasingly abusive.[33] The passage of time was to prove that the Macartney embassy had not paved the way for Lord Amherst's later mission. The verdict of history was categorically stated by the chronicler of the British East India Company: "The embassy failed in the business for which it had been dispatched to China."[34]

[31] Pindar, *Works*, IV, 236.
[32] *The Gentleman's Magazine*, LXIV (1794), 815.
[33] Pritchard, *The Crucial Years*, pp. 365–74; Morse, *Chronicles*, II, 255–76.
[34] Morse, *Chronicles*, II, 230.

The ambassador and his train felt some consolation perhaps in the subsequent downfall of the minister Ho-shen, long suspected as the archenemy of the British, after the death of Kien Long.[35] Macartney's reflection that the Chinese empire was long past the peak of her power and was relapsing into semi-barbarity[36] could not ameliorate the bitterness of the end of his mission. Doubtless he sympathized with Aeneas Anderson's blunt summation: "In short, we entered Pekin like paupers, we remained in it like prisoners, and we quitted it like vagrants."[37] The justice of his remark was underlined by the subsequent failure of Lord Amherst.[38]

It is, however, Macartney's embassy which marks a logical stopping place for this study of Anglo-Chinese relations. The failure of both sides to reach any sort of agreement indicates how little understanding had been achieved in the two centuries since Elizabeth had projected a trade mission to the Emperor. Europe and England had been inundated with narratives and reports, but China was little more understood than it had been in the days of Mandeville. In the course of the seventeenth and eighteenth centuries the Jesuits and pro-Chinese Europeans had constructed a detailed argument for the superiority of Chinese government and morality. Others had argued for their preeminence in the sciences. But little by little the legend had crumbled. During the latter part of the eighteenth century it had become virtually impossible to sift the fact from the rubble of the myth. The Utopia of the philosopher-kings had fallen in ruins.

[35]For biographies of Ho-shen and other Chinese and Manchus of the seventeenth and eighteenth century see Arthur W. Hummel, *Eminent Chinese of the Ch'ing Period*, 2 vols., Washington, 1943–44.

[36]Robbins, *Our First Ambassador*, p. 394.

[37]Aeneas Anderson, *A Narrative of the British Embassy to China* (Basle, 1795), pp. 222–23.

[38]Morse, *Chronicles*, III, 256–306; Collis, *The Great Within*, pp. 302–25.

Though nineteenth century scholars made much use of the work of earlier Sinologists, it was necessary to reappraise these earlier works carefully. Basic misconceptions and distortions had long persisted. Till the end of the seventeenth century Cathay had been generally believed a country to the west of China. At the time of Macartney's embassy a reckless group of Botany Bay convicts had attempted to escape to China, believing it to be separated from the Australian mainland by a mere hundred miles.[39] Knowledge of China's mystical religions and art was hopelessly muddled. Knowledge of its language was almost as confused. The Manchus had discouraged the English from its study, and, great scholar though he was, Sir William Jones, the foremost Orientalist, had realized that his attainments in Chinese were distinctly limited.[40]

With the beginning of the nineteenth century real English Sinology begins. In the preceding two hundred years a myth had evolved and been destroyed. It had been of value in fostering the idea of the cosmopolitan citizen of the world, in launching a singularly graceful type of art, in celebrating learning and morality in government, but it had harmed the cause of China in exalting that country to an unnatural degree. It had generated a counterwave of abuse. For almost two centuries Europe and England had known a China half real and half visionary. In the nineteenth century the panegyric and abuse still echoed.[41] But little by little genuine Oriental scholarship began to rebuild from the ruins. Only in the last century have scholars begun the all-important task of the sympathetic interpretation of the real China to the Western world.

[39]*The British Critic,* II (1793), 65.

[40]Lord Teignmouth, *Memoirs of the Life . . . of Sir William Jones* (London, 1835), II, 167–68.

[41]George C. Martin, "China in English Literature," *Asiatic Review,* n. s., XI (1917), 407–33, notes many references in nineteenth century English literature. Cf. Carlyle's tribute to China in "The Hero as a Man of Letters," with De Quincey's "The Opium Question with China in 1840" and "The Chinese Question in 1857."

INDEX